This book belongs to:

_____

Libra Daily Horoscope 2025

Author's Note: Time set to Coordinated Universal Time Zone (UT±0)

Mystic Cat
Suite 41906, 3/2237 Gold Coast HWY
Mermaid Beach, Queensland, 4218
Australia
islandauthor@hotmail.com

Contents

The 12 Zodiac Star Signs

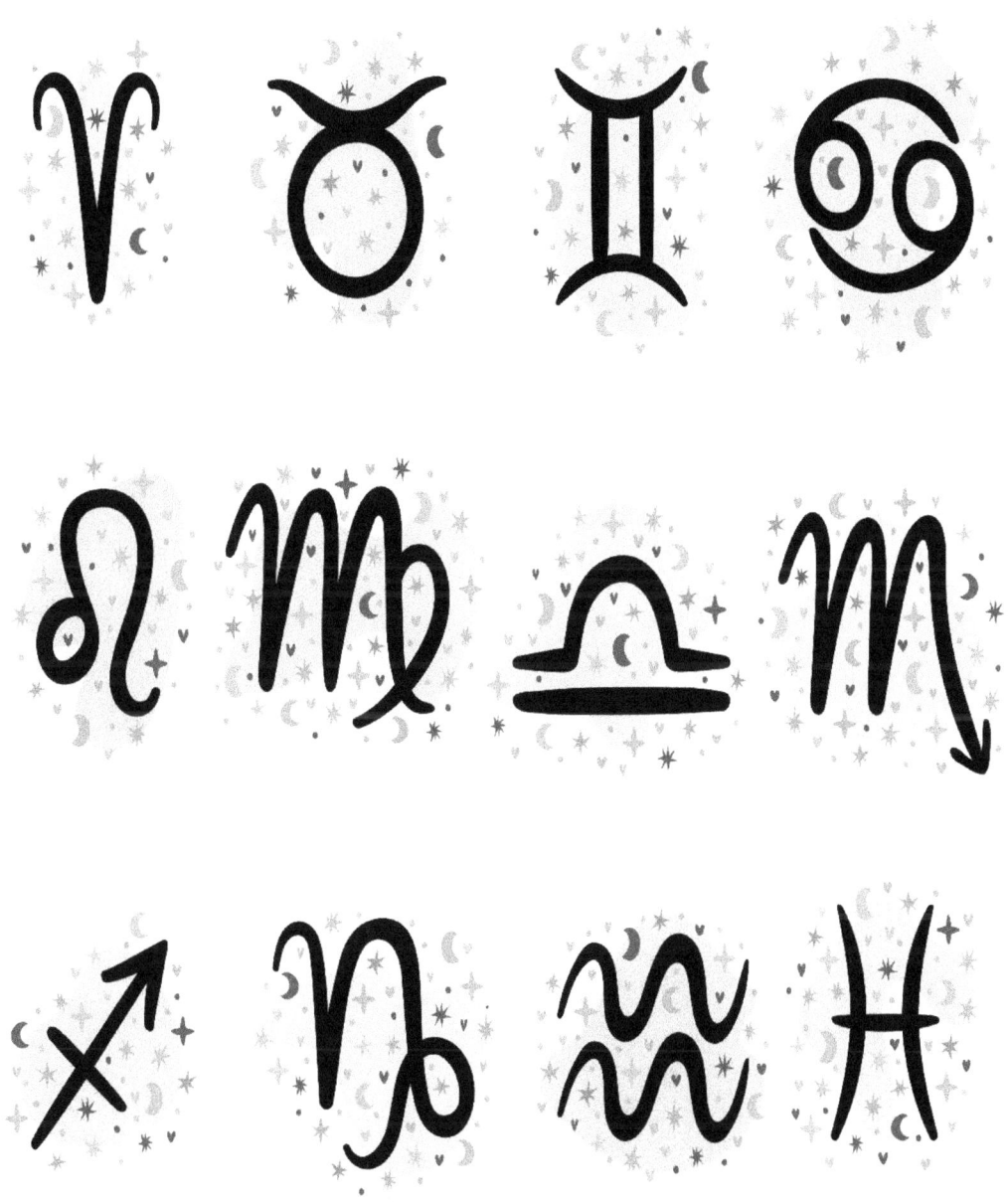

2025

January
S	M	T	W	T	F	S
			1	2	3	4
5	6	7	8	9	10	11
12	13	14	15	16	17	18
19	20	21	22	23	24	25
26	27	28	29	30	31	

February
S	M	T	W	T	F	S
						1
2	3	4	5	6	7	8
9	10	11	12	13	14	15
16	17	18	19	20	21	22
23	24	25	26	27	28	

March
S	M	T	W	T	F	S
						1
2	3	4	5	6	7	8
9	10	11	12	13	14	15
16	17	18	19	20	21	22
23	24	25	26	27	28	29
30	31					

April
S	M	T	W	T	F	S
		1	2	3	4	5
6	7	8	9	10	11	12
13	14	15	16	17	18	19
20	21	22	23	24	25	26
27	28	29	30			

May
S	M	T	W	T	F	S
				1	2	3
4	5	6	7	8	9	10
11	12	13	14	15	16	17
18	19	20	21	22	23	24
25	26	27	28	29	30	31

June
S	M	T	W	T	F	S
1	2	3	4	5	6	7
8	9	10	11	12	13	14
15	16	17	18	19	20	21
22	23	24	25	26	27	28
29	30					

July
S	M	T	W	T	F	S
		1	2	3	4	5
6	7	8	9	10	11	12
13	14	15	16	17	18	19
20	21	22	23	24	25	26
27	28	29	30	31		

August
S	M	T	W	T	F	S
					1	2
3	4	5	6	7	8	9
10	11	12	13	14	15	16
17	18	19	20	21	22	23
24	25	26	27	28	29	30
31						

September
S	M	T	W	T	F	S
	1	2	3	4	5	6
7	8	9	10	11	12	13
14	15	16	17	18	19	20
21	22	23	24	25	26	27
28	29	30				

October
S	M	T	W	T	F	S
			1	2	3	4
5	6	7	8	9	10	11
12	13	14	15	16	17	18
19	20	21	22	23	24	25
26	27	28	29	30	31	

November
S	M	T	W	T	F	S
						1
2	3	4	5	6	7	8
9	10	11	12	13	14	15
16	17	18	19	20	21	22
23	24	25	26	27	28	29
30						

December
S	M	T	W	T	F	S
	1	2	3	4	5	6
7	8	9	10	11	12	13
14	15	16	17	18	19	20
21	22	23	24	25	26	27
28	29	30	31			

2025

Daily Horoscope

LIBRA

As your astrologer, I wish to explain why one horoscope book may differ from another for each zodiac sign. The vast array of astrological activity constantly occurring in the sky requires me to focus on the essential aspect of the star sign I am writing for on any given day. Each zodiac sign is unique, and the various planetary factors affect them differently.

When crafting horoscopes, I pay special attention to the significant astrological aspects directly impacting a specific sign. By doing so, I can provide the most insightful and relevant guidance to individuals of that zodiac sign. While there might be multiple planetary alignments on a particular day, one aspect may hold more significance for a specific sign than others.

Considering the ruling planets and elements associated with each zodiac sign further refines my interpretations. This attention to detail ensures that the horoscope resonates with the distinct characteristics and tendencies of the star sign in question.

Ultimately, I aim to offer personalized insights and advice based on each zodiac sign's unique cosmic influences. By focusing on each star sign's most relevant astrological aspects, I can help readers better understand themselves and navigate the energies surrounding them. Embracing each zodiac sign's strengths, challenges, and opportunities allows me to create a horoscope book tailored to my readers' needs.

"We are born at a given moment, in a given place, and, like vintage years of wine, we have the qualities of the year and the season of which we are born. Astrology does not lay claim to anything more."

—Carl Jung

JANUARY

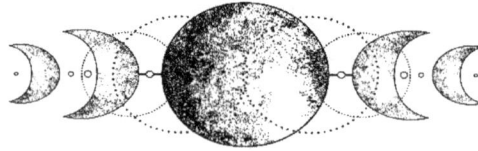

MOON MAGIC

Sun	Mon	Tue	Wed	Thu	Fri	Sat
			1	2	3	4
5	6	7	8	9	10	11
12	13	14	15	16	17	18
19	20	21	22	23	24	25
26	27	28	29	30	31	

New Moon

WOLF MOON

30 Monday

With the Moon ingress in Capricorn, a new lunar cycle begins, signaling a time of focus and determination in your life. You can set practical goals and work towards achieving them. You feel motivated to establish a solid foundation and to take on responsibilities with a structured approach. Planning, strategizing, and cultivating patience and perseverance are excellent during this time. This New Moon invites you to embrace a practical mindset and steadily progress toward your ambitions.

31 Tuesday

The universe echoes a call to proactivity and openness to new possibilities, akin to a tributary seeking the ocean. Your dreams, much like the watercourse, find their way into your life, and your active participation accelerates the process, making things happen sooner rather than later. Stay open to new leads, allowing the confluence of various elements to come together harmoniously. Dive into an enriching landscape, promoting harmony and happiness.

1 Wednesday

This New Year's Day, with the Moon ingress Aquarius, you enter a period of fresh perspectives and innovative thinking. This celestial alignment invites you to embrace individuality and ideas that challenge the status quo. It's a time to share your vision for a progressive and inclusive future. This Aquarian energy encourages you to break free from old patterns and embrace your unique qualities. It's an opportunity to foster community and contribute to positive change.

2 Thursday

You can initiate a bold new beginning in your life, marking a pivotal juncture to spread your wings and ascend toward rising aspects. Swift decisions ripple waves of transformation, elevating the potential available. The outlook shines with luck and luxury, promising enhanced security and stability. A side project aligned with your artistic inclinations taps into a reservoir of harmony and well-being. It heralds a fresh start, unleashing a cascade of opportunities.

JANUARY

3 Friday

With Venus entering Pisces, you may experience heightened compassion and empathy in your relationships. This transit invites you to connect on a deeper emotional level and seek harmony and understanding with others. It's an excellent time to express your love and affection through acts of kindness and selflessness. As Mars opposes Pluto, you might encounter intense power struggles and conflicts that challenge your assertiveness and drive.

4 Saturday

With the Sun sextile Saturn, you can bring discipline, focus, and structure into your life. This harmonious aspect allows you to align your ambitions and goals with a strong sense of responsibility and determination. You can set realistic and achievable targets, and your efforts will likely yield long-lasting and meaningful results. This aspect encourages you to take a mature and steady approach to your endeavors, ensuring that you lay down solid foundations for future success.

5 Sunday

With the Moon entering Aries, you may feel energy and enthusiasm propelling you forward. This fiery and assertive energy ignites your passion and drive, urging you to take decisive action to pursue your desires. You are ready to take on new challenges and assert your individuality. This transit encourages you to trust your instincts, embrace spontaneity, and fearlessly venture into new territories. You may find activities that require courage as you seek to assert your presence.

6 Monday

With Mars entering Cancer, you may notice a shift in your assertiveness and energy. This transition brings a more nurturing and sensitive approach to your actions and desires. Your passions channel towards creating a sense of emotional security and a harmonious home environment. This transit encourages a supportive and agreeable atmosphere. You may be more motivated to protect and care for your loved ones and create a sanctuary to retreat and recharge.

7 Tuesday

As the Moon enters Taurus, you may experience a sense of grounding and stability in your emotional state. This influence encourages you to focus on creating a harmonious and stable environment around you. You may find satisfaction in connecting with nature, enjoying good food, or indulging in activities that bring pleasure and serenity. It's a time to appreciate the physical world's beauty and abundance and find emotional fulfillment through material comforts.

8 Wednesday

With Mercury entering Capricorn, you can expect a shift in your thought processes and communication style. Your focus turns toward practicality, organization, and long-term planning. You may be inclined to think and speak in a structured and disciplined manner, seeking clarity and precision in your words. This influence encourages you to be more strategic and goal-oriented as you recognize the importance of practicality in achieving objectives.

9 Thursday

In the pursuit of your dreams, you initiate a journey that not only enhances your circumstances but also unravels magic and mayhem, infusing your spirit with newfound vigor. Within this transformative atmosphere, anticipate more options to redesign your journey, aligning it with the person you are becoming. The therapeutic aspect seeps into your surroundings, nurturing grounded foundations that provide a stable platform for your endeavors.

JANUARY

10 Friday

With the Moon entering Gemini, you may experience a heightened curiosity and intellectual stimulation. Your emotions become more adaptable and changeable, reflecting the dual nature of Gemini. You will likely feel more social and inclined to engage in conversations and interactions, enabling you to seek greater understanding. This transit encourages you to express your thoughts and feelings as communication becomes your focus.

11 Saturday

Adaptability enhances stability on the home front, nurturing a profound sense of well-being. Opportunities on the horizon bring bright blessings, emphasizing the development of new goals and dreams. The prospect of a change of scenery becomes therapeutic, offering a refreshing perspective that promotes happiness. Connections with supportive companions provide avenues for conversation and insightful ideas.

12 Sunday

With the Moon moving into Cancer, you will experience a deepening of emotions and a strong need for comfort and security. You may find yourself seeking solace in familiar environments and nurturing activities. This transit encourages you to connect with your inner self and your loved ones on a deeper emotional level. Your intuition and sensitivity heighten, allowing you to understand the unspoken needs and desires of those around you.

13 Monday

With the Sun forming a trine with Uranus and the Full Moon illuminating the sky, you are in for exciting breakthroughs and heightened awareness. The Sun trine Uranus aspect sparks a sense of individuality, freedom, and innovation. You may break free from old patterns, embrace your unique qualities, and explore new possibilities. This harmonious alignment between the Sun and Uranus encourages you to step outside your comfort zone and confidently embrace change.

14 Tuesday

With the Moon entering Leo and Venus forming a square with Jupiter, you are entering a period filled with passion, enthusiasm, and a desire for indulgence. The Moon's ingress into Leo brings a sense of confidence, creativity, and self-expression to your emotional landscape. You feel more inclined to express your unique personality and share your talents. However, the Venus square Jupiter aspect brings a tendency towards excess and overindulgence.

15 Wednesday

As significant changes unfold, infusing life with renewed energy, a lighter chapter emerges, nurturing abundance and happiness. Rising prospects encourage you to push against the barriers, prioritizing yourself to develop impactful goals that resonate with your essence. You soon discover a path that spotlights growth, advancement, and progression, nurturing your talents and reshaping your confidence and outlook on life.

16 Thursday

The Sun-opposed Mars aspect creates a push-pull dynamic between your sense of self-expression and your assertiveness. You may feel the urge to pursue your goals, but there could also be conflicts and power struggles that arise. Finding a healthy balance between passion and aggression is essential. Avoid unnecessary disputes and seek constructive outlets for your energy. As the Moon moves into Virgo, you are encouraged to focus on practicality and organization.

17 Friday

With the Sun sextile Neptune, you may immerse yourself in a sea of heightened intuition and creative inspiration. This aspect brings a harmonious connection between your conscious self and the realm of dreams, spirituality, and imagination. It allows you to tap into your inner wisdom and connect with a sense of higher purpose. You feel greater empathy and compassion towards others and a desire to contribute to the greater good.

18 Saturday

Anticipate transformative changes, ripe with opportunities to grow meaningfully. It heralds an enriching chapter, requiring you to set unique goals and fine-tune your visionary outlook. With a strategic plan in place, you trim away unfruitful aspects, paving the way for new endeavors that promise not just enrichment but also profound happiness. This strategic approach sets the tone for a refreshing period of expansion, where each step forward aligns with your evolving vision.

19 Sunday

The Mercury sextile Saturn and Mercury sextile Venus aspects add a touch of intellectual depth and communication skills to your interactions. It is a good time for expressing your thoughts and ideas clearly and in a structured way, making it easier to establish solid connections and understanding with others. You can appreciate your unique perspectives as the Sun enters Aquarius. By embracing these aspects, you foster meaningful relationships and communicate effectively.

20 Monday

As you grow and expand the borders of your life, new areas unfold, guiding you toward greener pastures. Sharing experiences with kindred spirits becomes an integral part of your routine, paving the way for an extensive phase of progress that opens up life in exciting dimensions. Your keen eye spots a fantastic opportunity that offers wide-ranging benefits. Expanding your social life connects you with companions who fuel insightful discussions and trailblazing thoughts.

21 Tuesday

As the Moon ingresses Scorpio, it amplifies transformative energies, bringing emotional depth and intensity to the forefront. You may find yourself drawn to introspection and exploring the deeper layers of your emotions. This transit is a period for embracing your emotional truth, healing emotional wounds, and gaining insights into your subconscious. You embark on self-discovery and empowerment as you navigate emotions and uncover hidden aspects.

22 Wednesday

Constructive dialogues carry news and information, cracking the code to expand your vision. It's an essential time for advancing life goals and developing skills. Working with your talents creates a robust foundation, becoming the bedrock of security in your world. You can pour your energy into a unique endeavor, creating a master plan as you climb towards your goals. It brings a fruitful direction to channel your energy, propelling you to a new level of learning.

23 Thursday

With Mars sextile Uranus, you may feel a surge of energy and a desire for change and excitement. It encourages you to embrace your individuality and take bold, innovative actions. It sparks a sense of adventure and the courage to break free from old routines. As Mercury opposes Mars, there can be a tendency for conflicts to arise in communication and mental pursuits. It's essential to be mindful of impulsive reactions and to find a balance between assertiveness and diplomacy.

24 Friday

With the Moon ingress Sagittarius, you may experience a sense of adventure and a desire for exploration. Your emotions offer optimism and a yearning for freedom. This transit encourages you to expand your mental and physical horizons as you seek new experiences and knowledge. You may feel a pull towards travel, higher learning, or philosophical pursuits. Your emotions fuel curiosity and a need for a greater understanding of the world around you.

25 Saturday

With Venus trine Mars, harmonious and passionate energy infuses your relationships and desires. You find yourself experiencing a delightful balance between love and assertiveness, blending romance with action. This aspect enhances your ability to attract and connect with others on both an emotional and physical level. Your charm and magnetism heighten, making expressing your desires and pursuing your passions easier.

26 Sunday

With the Moon ingress Capricorn, you enter a period of increased focus and determination. Your emotions are aligned with practicality and ambition, allowing you to progress toward your goals with a grounded approach. This lunar placement brings a sense of responsibility and discipline to your emotional state, helping you stay organized and structured in your pursuits. Mercury sextile Neptune further enhances your mental clarity and intuition.

27 Monday

Trust your gut instincts as a guiding light, navigating the path ahead with grace and flexibility. This approach grants you a deeper understanding of the blocks limiting progress. Adaptability and patience position you to grow the path, advancing into uncharted territory with newfound responsibilities and an upgraded working life. News arrives, providing the green light for this transformative phase.

28 Tuesday

As the Moon ingresses, Aquarius aligns with Mercury, and your emotions align with your intellectual pursuits. You experience objectivity in your emotional responses, allowing you to view situations from a broader perspective. You find it easier to approach emotional matters logically, seeking solutions and understanding through intellectual exploration. This lunar placement supports your ability to detach from biases and cultivates emotional independence.

29 Wednesday

With Mercury conjunct with Pluto, your thoughts and communication are more intense. This aspect brings a heightened sense of perception and the ability to uncover hidden truths and delve into the depths of any subject matter. You may draw profound and transformative conversations, seeking to understand the underlying motivations and dynamics. This transit encourages you to explore the depths of your mind and express your ideas with conviction and power.

30 Thursday

Uranus turns direct. Moon ingress Pisces. Sun trine Jupiter. Together, these aspects invite you to embrace change, follow your intuition, and embark on a journey of growth and expansion. Embrace the unexpected and trust in the flow of cosmic energies that support your journey toward greater authenticity, emotional depth, and the realization of your aspirations. Stay open and let your spirit soar as you step into the ever-unfolding tapestry of your life's journey.

FEBRUARY

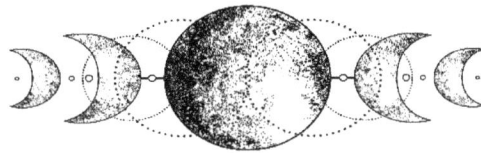

MOON MAGIC

Sun	Mon	Tue	Wed	Thu	Fri	Sat
						1
2	3	4	5	6	7	8
9	10	11	12	13	14	15
16	17	18	19	20	21	22
23	24	25	26	27	28	

NEW MOON

_____

_____

_____

_____

_____

_____

_____

_____

_____

_____

_____

_____

_____

_____

_____

_____

_____

_____

_____

SNOW MOON

31 Friday

Welcome the arrival of transformative news, unraveling fresh opportunities in the tapestry of your life. This revelation goes beyond the surface, offering you a panoramic view of significant possibilities that have been quietly circulating in the background. A side adventure extends its invitation, promising a unique trail that not only nurtures your existing abilities but also serves as a crucible for refining your talents.

1 Saturday

With Venus conjunct Neptune, you can immerse yourself in love, beauty, and imagination. This celestial alignment creates a dreamy and romantic atmosphere that awakens your heart and enhances your sensitivity to the subtle nuances of emotions and connections. You may find yourself drawn to artistic expressions, music, or spiritual practices that touch your soul. It's a time to indulge in the pleasures of love and cultivate compassion and empathy toward others.

2 Sunday

Moon ingress Aries. You may be more impulsive and eager to take risks, but remember to channel this energy wisely. Use this time to set clear intentions, pursue your passions, and embark on exciting endeavors that align with your desires. Trust your instincts and let the fiery energy of Aries propel you forward on your path of self-discovery and personal growth. Embrace the spirit of spontaneity and the thrill of stepping outside your comfort zone.

3 Monday

Mercury trine Jupiter is a good time for positive thinking, planning, and problem-solving. You have a keen sense of intuition and can trust your instincts when making decisions. Embrace this auspicious alignment by confidently expressing yourself and sharing your ideas with others. Your words carry wisdom and inspiration, and you have the potential to make a profound impact through your communication.

4 Tuesday

With the Moon moving into Taurus, Venus entering Aries, and Jupiter turning direct, energy shifts, bringing a renewed sense of stability, passion, and forward momentum into your life. The grounding influence of the Taurus Moon invites you to connect with your feelings, find comfort in the present moment, and nurture yourself in tangible and practical ways. Simultaneously, the entrance of Venus into fiery Aries sparks a sense of enthusiasm and independence.

5 Wednesday

Feel the subtle shifts as the wheels of change gain momentum, unveiling a spectrum of possibilities that beckon growth and advancement. Amidst this transformative landscape, a curious option emerges, drawing lighter energy into your sphere. This option becomes a breakthrough, guiding your efforts toward a grand, big-picture goal. The path ahead becomes a wellspring of abundance, and your penchant for creative exploration deepens, leading to a knowledge journey.

6 Thursday

With the Moon entering Gemini, a curious and versatile energy sweeps over you. Your mind becomes eager to explore new ideas and engage in stimulating conversations. This transit ignites your intellectual curiosity and encourages you to seek knowledge and expand your mental horizons. You find yourself drawn to social interactions and connecting with others on a mental level. Communication flows effortlessly, and you may express your thoughts and ideas eloquently.

7 Friday

Relationships take on a more intense and transformative quality as you delve into the deeper layers of connection and understanding. Personal empowerment and self-discovery run through relationships and the things you value. It encourages you to embrace love's transformative power and align your values with your desires. Embrace the opportunities for growth and self-realization as you navigate the powerful energies of Venus and Pluto working together in harmony.

8 Saturday

As the Moon moves into Cancer, you may experience heightened emotional sensitivity and nurturing energy. Your focus is creating a safe and comfortable environment where you can feel truly at home. This transit is a time to prioritize self-care and nourishment for yourself and those you care about. You may find yourself more attuned to your feelings and the needs of others, seeking to provide a supportive and nurturing presence.

9 Sunday

With the Sun in conjunction with Mercury, your mind is sharp, and your communication skills heighten. You can express yourself clearly and effectively, making it an ideal time for meaningful conversations, negotiations, or sharing your ideas with others. Meanwhile, the Mars trine Saturn aspect brings a harmonious blend of energy and discipline. You have the drive and determination to take focused action toward your goals.

10 Monday

As the Moon enters Leo, vibrant and expressive energy envelops your being. You fill with confidence and self-assuredness that shines brightly from within. This celestial shift brings out your natural flair for creativity and drama, urging you to embrace your unique talents and let your inner light illuminate the world around you. Your emotions become fiery and passionate, encouraging you to pursue your heart's desires and indulge in joyful self-expression.

11 Tuesday

When the Sun forms a square aspect with Uranus, you may experience a period of unexpected disruptions and a desire for greater freedom and independence. This aspect can bring sudden changes or surprises into your life, challenging the status quo and pushing you to break free from limiting patterns. You might feel a strong urge to rebel against authority or traditional expectations, seeking to express your individuality and embrace your unique path.

12 Wednesday

The Full Moon invites you to reflect on the intentions you set during the previous New Moon and evaluate the progress you've made. It's a potent moment to let go of what no longer serves you and embrace necessary changes. Emotions may run high, offering valuable insights and clarifying certain situations. Use this time to balance your inner desires and external circumstances, as the Full Moon encourages you to align your actions with your authentic self.

13 Thursday

Moon ingress Virgo. Pay attention to your health and well-being during this period, as Virgo's influence encourages self-care and mindful living. Use this time to assess and refine your goals, taking small steps towards improvement and growth. The Moon in Virgo enables you to be discerning and strive for excellence in everything you do. Embrace the practicality and precision of this lunar phase, and let it guide you toward a more organized and productive path.

14 Friday

As Mercury moves into Pisces, you may find a shift in your communication style and emotional expression. This transit encourages a more intuitive and compassionate approach to connecting with others. You may feel more attuned to the subtle nuances of emotions and have a greater capacity for empathy and understanding. Your words may take on a poetic and imaginative quality, allowing you to express your feelings with depth and sensitivity.

15 Saturday

As the Moon moves into Libra, you may notice a shift in your focus towards finding balance and harmony in your relationships and surroundings. You become more attuned to the needs and feelings of others, seeking fairness and cooperation in your interactions. This transit encourages fostering peace and creating a pleasant and aesthetically pleasing environment. You enjoy socializing, seeking companionship, and engaging in activities that promote cooperation.

16 Sunday

Now is an opportune time to gain a panoramic overview of your life, identifying areas where effective changes can unfold, leading to a more prosperous path. As life takes you in a new direction, part of this process involves leaving behind individuals not aligned with your future growth cycle. Trim away problematic aspects and focus on the most meaningful path, meticulously mapping out plans that capture the essence of manifestation, ushering in new possibilities.

17 Monday

As the sun takes its celestial throne, bask in its radiant energy. It is a time of self-discovery and empowerment. Trust in the brilliance of your inner light, allowing the cosmic rays of the sun to guide you toward personal fulfillment. Embrace your uniqueness, and let the warmth of the sun's energy infuse every aspect of your journey. Engage in stimulating conversations, express your thoughts with clarity, and explore new intellectual horizons.

18 Tuesday

As the Moon moves into Scorpio and the Sun enters Pisces, you may experience a deepening of emotions and a heightened sensitivity to the unseen realms. The Scorpio energy encourages you to delve beneath the surface and explore the depths of your feelings, allowing for transformation and introspection. This cosmic combination is when you might uncover hidden truths and gain insight into the deeper aspects of your psyche.

19 Wednesday

You receive positive feedback and light a path that nurtures your goals and dreams. Creative stirrings bring new artistic projects and endeavors to life. Working with your abilities promotes a pleasing result and aligns you with achieving higher success. The climate around you ripens and opens up a sunny aspect that attracts supportive discussions and fresh ideas. Options ahead help you reshape goals and initiate transformation in your life.

20 Thursday

Moon ingress Sagittarius, Mercury Square Jupiter is a time to engage in open-minded conversations and embrace intellectual growth. Allow yourself to explore new ideas and perspectives, but also be willing to question your assumptions and listen to different viewpoints. By harnessing the enthusiastic energy of Sagittarius and applying it with discernment and wisdom, you can navigate this period with a sense of purpose and intellectual growth.

21 Friday

Venus, the celestial artist of love, graces your relationships with a palette of harmonious hues. Whether it's the romantic dance, the camaraderie of friends, or the ties of family, Venus encourages mutual understanding and cooperation. Revel in the beauty of these connections, recognizing that harmonious relationships are the masterpieces that color your life. Tune into your feelings to guide you through the ebb and flow of life's emotional tapestry.

22 Saturday

As the Moon moves into Capricorn, you reveal a sense of grounding and practicality. Capricorn's influence encourages you to focus on your long-term goals and responsibilities, urging you to take a structured and disciplined approach to achieve success. This lunar transit highlights the importance of setting realistic ambitions and working diligently toward them. It's a time to prioritize your professional aspirations, establish solid foundations, and make progress.

23 Sunday

Neptune, the ethereal dreamweaver, beckons you into a realm of inspiration and creativity. Immerse yourself in the dreamy landscapes of art, spirituality, and the intangible beauty that surrounds you. This cosmic embrace encourages exploration of the mystical aspects of life, inviting you to find inspiration in the realms of imagination and the unseen. Embrace the metamorphosis, as this transformational phase brings you closer to the core of your authentic self.

24 Monday

As Mars turns direct, a surge of energy and forward momentum infuses your life. You feel driven and motivated, ready to take decisive action and pursue your goals with renewed vigor. The challenges and obstacles that may have held you back are gone, allowing you to move forward with greater clarity and purpose. This planetary shift empowers you to assert yourself, assert your boundaries, and make bold choices that align with your authentic desires.

25 Tuesday

As the Moon moves into Aquarius, you may seek independence and individuality. This lunar transit encourages you to embrace your uniqueness and express your ideas in a way that challenges conventional thinking. Meanwhile, the alignment of Mercury with Saturn brings a focused and disciplined mindset to your communication and thinking processes. You are encouraged to approach your thoughts and conversations with a sense of responsibility and practicality.

26 Wednesday

As you expand your life, you open doors that grow the potential around your world. A happy event head brings rising potential into your social life. It beautifully orients you towards deepening personal bonds. It brings inspiration and energy, which spark positive change as you share with kindred spirits. Engaging with a broader essence of potential offers a bright and breezy time shared with people you value.

27 Thursday

As the Moon moves into Pisces, you feel a heightened intuition and emotional sensitivity. It is a time when your imagination and creativity elevate, allowing you to tap into the deeper realms of your subconscious. You may find yourself more attuned to spiritual or metaphysical insights, seeking meaning and connection in the world around you. The sextile between Mercury and Uranus adds exciting and innovative energy to your thoughts and communication.

MARCH

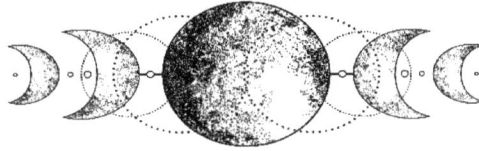

MOON MAGIC

Sun	Mon	Tue	Wed	Thu	Fri	Sat
						1
2	3	4	5	6	7	8
9	10	11	12	13	14	15
16	17	18	19	20	21	22
23	24	25	26	27	28	29
30	31					

New Moon

WORM MOON

_____

_____

_____

_____

_____

_____

_____

_____

_____

_____

_____

_____

_____

_____

_____

_____

_____

_____

_____

_____

28 Friday

Embrace the energy of the New Moon as it invites you to envision the future you desire and take the necessary steps to bring it to fruition. This transit is a potent time for self-reflection, introspection, and aligning intentions with your authentic self. Embrace the blank canvas before you and trust in the possibilities. Use the energy of the New Moon to ignite your passions, set clear intentions, and take inspired action toward creating the life you envision.

1 Saturday

With the Moon's ingress into Aries, this cosmic shift ignites a spark within you, fueling your passions and propelling you into action. You feel renewed self-confidence and assertiveness, ready to tackle challenges head-on. The Aries energy encourages you to embrace your individuality and take the initiative in pursuing your goals and dreams. It is a time to trust your instincts, follow your inner fire, and fearlessly step into new beginnings.

2 Sunday

As Venus turns retrograde, this period invites introspection and reflection on love, relationships, and values. You may find yourself reassessing the dynamics in your connections and examining your desires and needs. With Mercury conjunct Neptune, your imagination and intuition heighten, allowing for deep insights and creative inspiration. It is a time to trust your inner voice and explore the realms of dreams and spiritual understanding.

3 Monday

As Mercury ingresses Aries, your communication style becomes more direct, assertive, and spontaneous. You may speak your mind more confidently and take swift action on your ideas and plans. This energy encourages you to be bold and courageous in expressing yourself, sharing your opinions, and initiating conversations. With the Moon's ingress into Taurus, you are grounded and focused on stability and practical matters.

4 Tuesday

You embark on a journey where rising prospects loom ample, signaling opportunities that beckon you to foster growth in your world. Progression becomes an inevitable companion as you break new ground, investing your time and energy with unwavering commitment. The rewards of your actions align you in a better position as balanced and stable foundations emerge from a positive influence.

5 Wednesday

As the Moon enters Gemini, your mind becomes curious, adaptable, and open to new experiences. You feel a surge of mental energy and a desire to explore various ideas and perspectives. This lunar transit encourages you to engage in stimulating conversations, gather information, and expand your knowledge. With Mercury forming a sextile aspect to Pluto, your communication becomes insightful. You can delve into the core of matters, uncovering the underlying dynamics.

6 Thursday

Focusing on the basics takes you towards improving the foundations in your life. As you peel back the layers, you reveal refreshing potential that revolutionizes your life. It lets you proactively nurture your environment and harness the power of manifestation to achieve a pleasing result. It underscores an atmosphere of personal growth that puts you on a path toward growing your life. You reveal a journey ripe with potential and ready to blossom.

7 Friday

Moon ingress Cancer. It's a time to nurture and care for yourself and extend that to others. Trust your instincts and allow your empathic nature to guide you as you navigate the ebb and flow of your emotions. Embrace the power of home and family, finding solace and support in your closest relationships. Allow the Moon in Cancer to help you cultivate a sense of emotional well-being and create a sanctuary of love and warmth within your life.

8 Saturday

Your energy levels are high, and you can overcome obstacles and make things happen. It's important to channel this dynamic energy constructively and focus on activities that align with your passions and aspirations. Whether pursuing a personal goal, asserting your ideas, or engaging in physical activities, the Sun trine Mars empowers you to take charge and make significant progress. Embrace this powerful synergy and let it fuel your ambitions and propel you toward success.

9 Sunday

Moon ingress Leo is a time to embrace and share your inner light with others. Let your passion and enthusiasm guide you in pursuing activities that bring you joy and fulfillment. Allow your authentic self to shine brightly, inspiring those around you with your magnetic presence. Embrace the playful and generous spirit of Leo, and let it fuel your emotional landscape with warmth and positivity. Step into the spotlight and embrace your inner light with passion and enthusiasm.

10 Monday

Changes ahead enable you to cultivate magic and possibility. Many new options are coming that help you turn a corner and grow life in a new direction. Creativity and inspiration surge in your world as you hone in on a higher sense of purpose. The energy of manifestation blends with your aspirations to bring a vibrant landscape of potential. It brings grounded foundations that nurture well-being and happiness. It gives you a chance to reinvent your abilities and grow your talents.

11 Tuesday

When Mercury aligns with Venus, you experience a harmonious blend of communication and love. Your words infuse with charm and grace, making it easier for you to express your affection and connect with others on a deeper level. This alignment enhances your ability to convey your feelings with clarity and sincerity. Your interactions with loved ones are characterized by warmth and understanding, as you find it easier to express your appreciation and affection.

12 Wednesday

As the Moon enters Virgo and the Sun aligns with Saturn in conjunction, you hold an opportunity for focused determination and practicality. This cosmic combination urges you to approach your responsibilities with discipline and structure. You may desire to organize your life, set clear goals, and diligently work toward them. This alignment emphasizes the importance of taking a systematic approach to your tasks and paying attention to the details.

13 Thursday

You find that an area on the back burner for a while gets a shift forward. It sets the growth stage and leads to new adventures that draw excitement and fun. It emphasizes expansion as an exciting vista that tempts you forward. Embracing a life-affirming area brings well-being and grounded foundations. It offers a chance to push back the barriers that limit progress as you get involved in expanding your situation. Life becomes brighter and greener as new possibilities get you thinking.

14 Friday

Full Moon. Sun sextile Uranus. Moon ingress Libra. With the Moon's ingress into Libra, there is an emphasis on harmony, diplomacy, and cooperation. Finding balance in your interactions and cultivating fairness and understanding in your relationships becomes essential. You may seek compromise and find common ground, fostering connections based on mutual respect and shared values. It invites you to nurture harmonious relationships that contribute to well-being.

15 Saturday

When Mercury turns retrograde, it brings you a period of reflection and introspection. This celestial event invites you to slow down and review various aspects of your life. It's a time to reassess your communication style, relationships, and plans. Be mindful of potential misunderstandings and delays in communication during this phase. It's an opportunity to revisit unfinished tasks, reconnect with old friends, and tie up loose ends.

16 Sunday

Unexpected news arrives out of the blue, but it heads your life toward an upswing as new possibilities attract a lighter flow of energy around your life. You tap into a journey that inspires change, and it has you feeling optimistic about prospects. It emphasizes a time of fresh beginnings that connects you with a happy and enterprising landscape. It lets you chart a course towards sharing an enriching time with friends and companions.

17 Monday

When the Moon ingresses Scorpio, you delve into your emotions and explore your innermost desires. This transit is a time of intensity and passion, where you can embrace the transformative power within you. You may experience heightened sensitivity and intuition, allowing you to uncover hidden truths and gain profound insights. It's important to honor and acknowledge your emotions during this period, even if they seem intense or uncomfortable.

18 Tuesday

A new cycle emerges in your life that launches an exciting direction. A time of creativity and innovation helps build your talents and advance skills in new areas. You make notable tracks on growing your career path as you transition towards unique possibilities that promote growth. It secures a stable and grounded platform from which to grow your world. Remarkable changes on the horizon give you the green light to expand your life outwardly.

19 Wednesday

As the Moon enters Sagittarius, it ignites a sense of adventure and expansion within you. You may feel a strong urge to explore new physical and mental horizons. This lunar transit encourages you to embrace a broader perspective and seek higher truths. Combined with the Sun's conjunction with Neptune, there is a heightened sense of imagination and spiritual connection. You may draw mystical experiences or spiritual practices that nourish your soul.

20 Thursday

A new cycle begins as the Sun enters Aries and marks the Vernal Equinox. Aries, the first sign of the zodiac, ignites your spirit and sparks your enthusiasm. It is a time of action, initiative, and self-discovery. You feel a surge of vitality and a desire to assert yourself in the world. The Vernal Equinox further amplifies this energy, symbolizing a balance between day and night, light and darkness. It's a time to embrace your power and take courageous steps toward your goals.

21 Friday

With the combined energies of Venus and Pluto, you can experience profound emotional healing and growth, allowing you to let go of what no longer serves you and embrace the transformative power of love. It encourages you to explore your passions and desires and create profound and lasting connections with others. Open yourself to the transformative energy of Venus sextile Pluto, and allow it to guide you toward more profound levels of love and personal growth.

22 Saturday

Capricorn is an earth sign associated with ambition, structure, and pursuing long-term goals. You will likely feel more determined and driven to achieve your objectives during this lunar transition. You may find yourself prioritizing your work, career, or other areas of responsibility. It is a time for grounding your emotions and taking a practical approach to challenges. You may also feel a more substantial need for structure and organization.

23 Sunday

With the Sun sextile Pluto, you possess a powerful transformative energy that empowers you to make positive changes in your life. You can tap into your inner strength and uncover hidden depths within yourself. This alignment encourages you to embrace personal growth, assert your power, and create a meaningful impact in the world. Trust your abilities and let your radiant energy shine brightly, influencing and inspiring those around you.

24 Monday

When the Moon ingresses Aquarius, and the Sun conjoins Mercury, you may experience a desire to explore new ideas and perspectives. Aquarius is an air sign known for its innovative and unconventional nature, and it encourages you to think outside the box and embrace your individuality. With the Sun and Mercury coming together, your communication skills heighten, and you may find it easier to express your thoughts and opinions with clarity and confidence.

25 Tuesday

When Mercury sextiles Pluto, you have the potential to tap into deep insights and uncover hidden truths. This aspect brings a powerful blend of intellect and intuition, allowing you to discover profound understanding beneath the surface. Your mind is sharp and perceptive, enabling you to grasp complex concepts and engage in transformative conversations. You possess a natural curiosity and the ability to investigate and analyze precisely.

26 Wednesday

When the Moon enters Pisces, you may experience a shift in your emotional landscape. This transit invites you to embrace your intuitive and compassionate nature. You may feel attuned to the needs and emotions of others, offering a listening ear and a supportive presence. Your imagination heightens, allowing you to tap into creativity and spiritual exploration. It's a time to engage in self-care and introspection, nurturing your soul and connecting with your innermost desires.

27 Thursday

Black Moon ingress Scorpio. Venus ingress Pisces. Venus conjunct Neptune. You may find solace in creative expression, romantic experiences, or spiritual practices that nourish your spirit. Allow yourself to follow the currents of your emotions as they reveal profound truths and insights. Embrace the enchantment of this cosmic dance and let the transcendent energies of Pisces and Scorpio awaken. Trust in the transformative power of love and surrender to the divine flow of the universe.

28 Friday

Moon ingress Aries is a time to trust your instincts and follow your passions as you embrace the spirit of independence and self-discovery. Allow the Aries energy to fuel your drive and ambition, and let your enthusiasm and determination propel you forward. This lunar transit encourages you to embrace individuality and assert your needs and desires. Embrace the fiery power of Aries and let it ignite the spark within you as you fearlessly pursue your goals and dreams.

29 Saturday

As the New Moon graces the skies, you have a powerful opportunity for new beginnings and fresh starts. It is a time of intention-setting and planting the seeds of your dreams. It's a time to let go of the past and release any limitations that have held you back. Set clear intentions and take inspired action towards your goals. It is a potent time to manifest your desires and create positive change. Trust your inner wisdom and intuition as you navigate this new lunar cycle.

30 Sunday

It's a time to embrace your inner vision and tap into the subtler realms of consciousness. With Neptune transitioning into Aries and the Moon moving into Taurus, you are encouraged to ground these ethereal energies into practical and tangible expressions. Trust your intuition and allow your thoughts to flow freely, for you can discover innovative solutions and insights in this space of creative fluidity.

APRIL

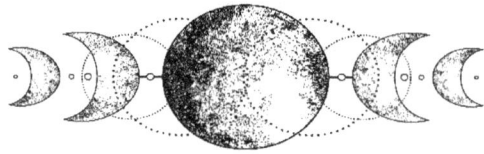

MOON MAGIC

Sun	Mon	Tue	Wed	Thu	Fri	Sat
		1	2	3	4	5
6	7	8	9	10	11	12
13	14	15	16	17	18	19
20	21	22	23	24	25	26
27	28	29	30			

NEW MOON

PINK MOON

_____

_____

_____

_____

_____

_____

_____

_____

_____

_____

_____

_____

_____

_____

_____

_____

_____

_____

_____

_____

31 Monday

You have the hunger to drive your goals forward. Information emerges, and this news lets you get inspired by something larger than yourself. It brings a source of energy that offers a mission you feel excited about developing. Exploring new options in your life lets you take the reins and head towards growth. Your patience and perseverance help you grow your dreams. A curious assignment comes calling, which speeds up the level of learning and development in your life.

1 Tuesday

As the Moon enters Gemini, your mind becomes agile and curious, ready to explore new ideas and engage in lively conversations. This lunar shift encourages you to embrace your intellectual side and seek stimulating experiences that expand your perspective. Embrace Gemini's playful and inquisitive nature as you explore different perspectives and expand your knowledge. Perfect for social interactions, seeking connections, and meaningful social exchanges.

2 Wednesday

A new approach brings lightness and happiness to your door. It brings discovery and personal growth, which helps you move forward toward developing areas that speak to your soul. Your creativity rises as you transition to learning new areas. It brings a chance to reinvent life and nurture a wellspring of possibility in your world. It offers a busy time that launches your talents towards advancement. Working with your skills opens the floodgates to rising potential.

3 Thursday

As the Moon enters Cancer, you may feel a gentle wave of emotional sensitivity and nurturing energy. This lunar transit invites you to honor and embrace your emotions, creating a space for self-care and nurturing. Your intuition and empathy heighten, allowing you to connect deeply with your feelings and the emotions of those around you. It's a time to prioritize self-care and create a supportive environment that nurtures your emotional well-being.

4 Friday

As Saturn sextiles Uranus and Mars also form a sextile with Uranus, you may feel a powerful blend of stability and innovation. This harmonious alignment between the planets brings a unique opportunity for you to embrace structure and change. You navigate challenges and opportunities with confidence and adaptability. With Saturn's grounding influence and Uranus's innovative energy, you can channel your ambition and determination toward meaningful endeavors.

5 Saturday

The Mars-Saturn trine encourages you to take calculated risks in a measured and controlled manner. It is a time to establish a solid foundation for your endeavors and demonstrate your resilience and determination. Trust in your abilities, stay committed to your objectives, and let the supportive energy of this aspect guide you towards long-lasting achievements. Remember to pace yourself and maintain a healthy balance between work and rest, allowing you to sustain your efforts.

6 Sunday

The Venus-Mars trine adds a touch of passion and harmony to your relationships and creative endeavors. This alignment fuels your desires, ignites your creativity, and encourages you to express your affection and desires authentically and enthusiastically. Embrace the joyful energy of the Moon in Leo, the Sun sextile Jupiter, and the Venus trine Mars. Let them inspire you to shine your light brightly, embrace abundance, and cultivate meaningful connections with others.

7 Monday

With Mercury turning direct, any previous communication issues or misunderstandings improve. This shift can bring clarity to your thoughts, enhance your ability to express yourself effectively and support smoother interactions in your daily life. It's an excellent time to move forward with plans, make important decisions, and engage in open and honest dialogue. Trust you can create more stable and balanced connections in your relationships.

8 Tuesday

When Venus forms a sextile with Uranus, it brings an exciting and unexpected flavor to your relationships and personal expression. You may be attracted to unique and unconventional individuals or experiences that stimulate your sense of adventure and freedom. This aspect encourages you to embrace spontaneity and break free from old patterns, allowing for vital connections. As the Moon moves into Virgo, you can focus on practical matters and details of daily life.

9 Wednesday

A favorable aspect cracks the code to a brighter chapter. You become involved with a venture that takes on a curious light as it draws new friendships into your circle. It brings the gift of companionship as you chart a course toward advancing your abilities. You discover room to spread your wings and open up a social path that nurtures happiness and well-being. Attractive possibilities emerge that further progress your vision towards new options.

10 Thursday

Creativity rises, bringing lightness into your life as you implement strategies to nurture well-being and happiness in your world. It gives you a chance to launch your talents into an area that promotes your skills. News surfaces that help you make effective changes and grow your life in the direction of your own making. It brings a time for upgrading dreams and chasing goals as you thrive in a more social and connected environment.

11 Friday

Moon ingress Libra is a time to improve your social connections, engage in meaningful conversations, and explore the beauty of art, culture, and aesthetics. The Moon in Libra invites you to embrace the qualities of diplomacy, grace, and cooperation as you navigate the world around you, promoting harmony and fostering understanding in your interactions with others. You can enhance your relationships by cultivating balance and fairness in your interactions.

12 Saturday

Changes ahead bring expansion to the forefront of your life. It brings a more social aspect that offers lively activities and a sense of connection and support with friends. It brings a relaxing time shared with kindred spirits who provide thoughtful discussions and innovative ideas. As your social life heats up with new potential, it has you feeling lighter and more connected with the vibrant side of life. It creates an excellent environment for nurturing and deepening friendships.

13 Sunday

As the Full Moon illuminates the night sky, you may feel a heightened intensity and emotional depth within yourself. This lunar phase brings a sense of culmination and fulfillment, allowing you to gain clarity and insight into various aspects of your life. With Venus turning direct, there is a shift in relationships, love, and values. You experience momentum and resolution in matters of the heart and a renewed appreciation for the things that bring you joy and pleasure.

14 Monday

Life brings remarkable opportunities that set you on a refreshing trend to grow your world. It helps you create a strong foundation that offers room to progress life forward into new areas. Being receptive to change attracts options that facilitate growth, learning, and advancement. Fortune aligns to form a clear window of opportunity that expands your horizons. It attracts a productive environment with a positive aspect that nurtures your abilities and craftsmanship.

15 Tuesday

You soon hit your stride in a new chapter of growth. Removing the heaviness and pushing back the barriers brings a lighter chapter that nurtures your abilities and grows your talents. You hit the road running and soon advance towards an inspiring time of increasing your skills and taking in new areas for development. It marks a bold beginning, transforming life as you build stable foundations that offer progression.

16 Wednesday

As the Moon enters Sagittarius, your spirit ignites with a sense of adventure and a thirst for knowledge. You can expand your horizons, both intellectually and experientially. This lunar transit encourages you to embrace new perspectives, explore different cultures, and seek opportunities for personal growth. Meanwhile, Mercury's ingress into Aries infuses your mind with a fiery energy that fuels your thoughts and communication style.

17 Thursday

When Mercury aligns with Neptune in conjunction, you are immersed in a world of imagination and heightened intuition. Your thoughts and communication take on a dreamy quality as your mind attunes to the subtle nuances of symbolism and hidden meanings. This alignment encourages you to tap into your creative faculties and explore the realms of poetry, art, and spirituality. Your intuition heightens, allowing you to perceive things beyond the surface level.

18 Friday

As Mars moves into Leo, you may feel confident and assertive. Your passions and desires are fueled by Leo's fiery energy, inspiring you to take bold action and pursue your goals with vigor. You radiate a magnetic charisma that draws others to you, and your leadership qualities shine brightly. With the Moon in Capricorn, your emotions become focused and disciplined, allowing you to tackle challenges with a practical and determined approach.

19 Saturday

As the Sun enters the grounded sign of Taurus, it illuminates your life with stability and a solid connection to the physical world. You find yourself drawn to the beauty of nature and the pleasures of the senses, seeking comfort and security in the material realm. Simultaneously, the harmonious trine between Mars and Neptune infuses your actions with a compassionate and inspired energy. Your imagination rises, allowing you to pursue your goals creatively and purposefully.

20 Sunday

As Easter Sunday dawns, you feel a sense of renewal and awakening. With the Moon's ingress into Aquarius, your emotions infuse with intellectual curiosity. You draw new ideas, connect with like-minded individuals, and embrace the spirit of innovation. Allow this potent combination of energies to inspire you to break free from old patterns, expand your consciousness, and embrace the power of transformation in all areas of your life.

21 Monday

In the cosmic dance of celestial energies, the Sun square Mars brings a potent and dynamic influence into your life. This alignment ignites a fiery and assertive fuel within you, urging you to take action and pursue your goals with vigor and determination. However, it has potential conflict and challenges, as the Sun's radiant power clashes with Mars' assertive drive. It is important to channel this energy wisely, balancing ambition and patience.

22 Tuesday

Information arrives, which gains your attention. It helps you leave the drama behind and turn the page on a fresh chapter in your social life. Getting involved with expanding life draws a pleasing result. Inspiration and creativity flow into your world to contribute new options that nurture happiness. You chart a course forward to a more balanced and contented environment. Sharing thoughtful dialogues with friends replenishes emotional tanks.

23 Wednesday

As the Moon glides into Pisces, a realm of dreams, intuition, and sensitivity, you may find yourself navigating emotional depths and seeking more profound understanding. However, the Sun square Pluto adds a layer of intensity and potential power struggles to the mix. This cosmic configuration invites you to delve into the hidden corners of your psyche, exploring the shadow aspects of your personality and confronting any fears or control issues that may arise.

24 Thursday

News arrives that brings new options to your door. It draws opportunities to connect with your broader social environment. It gives you a firm base from which to grow your world outwardly. Expanding your circle of friends brings liveliness and excitement, which hit a high note in your life. Nurturing companionship draws happiness and harmony, and this becomes the foundation from which you move forward in life.

25 Friday

Venus conjunct Saturn. Moon ingress Aries. This combination can bring a sense of determination and ambition to your interactions as you strive to balance your desires for security and independence. Finding a healthy equilibrium between your need for stability and your passion for personal freedom is essential. Allow yourself to assert your needs and desires while also being considerate of the needs and boundaries of others.

26 Saturday

Opportunity comes knocking and brings new people into your circle of friends. It offers a positive aspect that sees the rhythm and pace of life pick up. Harmony and abundance flow into your social life, providing a good sense of connection. Spending time with kindred spirits lays the groundwork for a balanced and happy chapter. It helps you tap into opportunities to grow and evolve your life in new directions. You discover a journey that holds promise.

27 Sunday

As Mars opposes Pluto, you may feel a heightened intensity and power struggle within yourself and your interactions with others. This aspect brings a clash between assertiveness and control, potentially leading to conflicts or power dynamics. It's essential to be mindful of any tendencies towards manipulation or power plays within yourself and your relationships. Remember that true strength lies in finding a harmonious balance and respecting the boundaries of others.

MAY

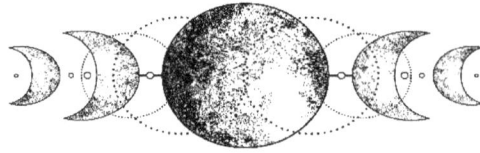

MOON MAGIC

Sun	Mon	Tue	Wed	Thu	Fri	Sat
				1	2	3
4	5	6	7	8	9	10
11	12	13	14	15	16	17
18	19	20	21	22	23	24
25	26	27	28	29	30	31

New Moon

Flower Moon

28 Monday

Experimenting with new pathways brings an upward trend that promotes advancement in your working life. It offers an uptick of potential that becomes a source of prosperity as you create progress in developing a meaningful goal in your life. A theme of improving circumstances cracks the code to a brighter chapter. You reap the rewards of new options, which open a path of change, growth, and success.

29 Tuesday

Moon enters Gemini; it is a time to embrace versatility and adaptability in your thoughts and communication. Your mind will likely be agile and receptive to new ideas, making it an excellent opportunity to engage in stimulating conversations and gather diverse perspectives. Gemini's influence encourages you to express yourself eloquently and with wit while also enabling you to remain open-minded and receptive to the ideas of others.

30 Wednesday

As Venus enters Aries, you may feel a surge of passion and assertiveness in your relationships and personal endeavors. The energy of Aries infuses your interactions with a bold and fiery spirit, inspiring you to take the lead and pursue what you desire. You become more direct in matters of the heart, unafraid to express your desires and stand up for your needs. This transit encourages you to embrace spontaneity and take action in love, creativity, and self-expression.

1 Thursday

Cancer, a water sign ruled by the Moon, invites you to dive deep into your emotions and seek comfort and security in familiar spaces. You may experience a greater need for nurturing and self-care during this time and a heightened sense of empathy and compassion toward others. Your intuition lets you tune into the needs and feelings of those around you. Take the opportunity to connect with your emotions, honor your needs, and find solace in embracing the familiar.

2 Friday

When Venus aligns with Neptune in conjunction, you may find yourself immersed in a world of beauty, imagination, and compassion. This celestial combination invites you to explore love, creativity, and spiritual connection. Your heart may open up to greater empathy and understanding, allowing you to see the divine essence in others. You might feel drawn to artistic pursuits or inspired to express your emotions creatively.

3 Saturday

When the Moon enters Leo, you may feel a surge of confidence and self-expression within you. Your inner light shines brightly, and you're ready to share your unique talents and creativity. This lunar transit ignites a sense of playfulness and encourages you to embrace your inner child. You may seek attention and the spotlight and bask in the admiration of others. Your emotions are passionate and fiery, fueling your desire for self-expression and the pursuit of joy.

4 Sunday

When Pluto turns retrograde, you may experience a profound inner transformation and introspection. This astrological event invites you to delve into the depths of your subconscious and examine the hidden aspects of your psyche. It's a time of soul-searching and uncovering buried emotions, fears, and desires. You may question old belief systems and patterns, seeking greater understanding and personal growth.

MAY

5 Monday

When Mercury forms a sextile aspect with Jupiter, you will likely experience intellectual curiosity and expanded thinking. This planetary alignment enhances your ability to absorb knowledge, communicate effectively, and express your ideas enthusiastically and optimistically. Your mind is open to new possibilities, and you draw learning, studying, or engaging in meaningful conversations. Share your thoughts and insights, and engage in positive and uplifting communication.

6 Tuesday

When Venus forms a sextile aspect with Pluto, you may experience a deepening of your emotional connections and a transformative influence on your relationships. This harmonious alignment brings intensity and passion to your romantic encounters, friendships, and partnerships. You may feel a strong attraction to others, and your interactions offer profound emotional depth and understanding.

7 Wednesday

Good news arrives and opens a pathway that grows your world. Improvements ahead offer an uplifting aspect that opens a pivotal time for developing long-term goals. You discover a new joy in life with the wind beneath your wings. Designing and developing your dreams promotes a bustling and productive environment that taps into advancement. Your efforts to improve circumstances open a bountiful journey that offers a rewarding result.

8 Thursday

Moon ingress Libra is a good time for socializing, networking, and connecting. You may also feel a heightened appreciation for beauty and aesthetics, seeking out aesthetically pleasing environments and engaging in creative pursuits. Use this time to cultivate balance within yourself and your relationships, and strive for harmonious interactions with others. Trust your intuition and seek out the beauty and harmony that surrounds you.

MAY

9 Friday

Your social life heads on an upswing and brings companionship your way. As things fall into place, it offers a journey of happiness that reboots and rejuvenates your energy. You link up with people who support your growth and evolution, and this fascinating aspect brings a focus on an expansion that feels adventurous and exciting. You connect with others who share your take on life, and this brings a new journey ahead.

10 Saturday

As Mercury moves into Taurus and the Moon enters Scorpio, you may experience a shift in your mental and emotional energies. Mercury in Taurus makes your thinking grounded and practical, focusing on tangible and reliable information. You find comfort in routine and prefer a measured approach to communication and decision-making. Meanwhile, the Moon in Scorpio intensifies your emotions, encouraging a delve into feelings and exploring your psyche's depths.

11 Sunday

News arrives that draws rejuvenation as sharing thoughts brings a therapeutic influence that improves circumstances. Unwrapping the way ahead brings a pleasant surprise that promotes happiness. Themes of abundance, security, and joy resonate throughout your life. An emphasis on your home life builds a stable and secure foundation. Life becomes more settled as a positive influence flows into your life.

MAY

12 Monday

As the Moon reaches its peak illumination, you may feel a sense of intensity and a need for deep reflection. However, this Full Moon faces a challenge between Mercury and Pluto, which can bring about intense mental energy and power struggles. As conflicts and misunderstandings can arise, be mindful of your thoughts and communication during this time. Take this opportunity to embrace the transformative power of this cosmic interplay.

13 Tuesday

Moon ingress Sagittarius astrological transit invites you to explore new horizons and broaden your perspective. Your focus may shift towards seeking higher truths, embarking on intellectual or spiritual pursuits, and embracing a more optimistic outlook. Sagittarius is a fiery and enthusiastic sign, encouraging you to pursue your passions with freedom and curiosity. It's a time to explore different belief systems, engage in philosophical discussions, and embark on learning journeys.

14 Wednesday

You are currently in a time of transition that can feel unsettling. Things are on the move for your life soon. It highlights a journey forward that brings growth, advancement, and progress. The essence of manifestation gently shifts your focus toward developing your vision for future development. Exploring new leads opens a journey of discovery that brings goodness to the surface of your life. Following your intuition draws an off-beaten track that deepens your knowledge.

15 Thursday

As the Moon moves into Capricorn, you may notice a shift in your emotional landscape. The energy of Capricorn brings a sense of grounding and practicality to your emotions, urging you to take a more disciplined and structured approach. You may focus on your long-term goals and responsibilities, seeking stability and security in your endeavors. This transit is a time to assess your ambitions and set realistic plans.

16 Friday

An emphasis on your social life draws a happy time as you create a path towards mingling with friends. You reveal new options around your social life, opening the door to a fresh start. Invitations and surprise get-togethers bring spontaneous opportunities to network and connect with your broader social environment. Sharing with kindred spirits sets the tone for a social phase that draws joy into your surroundings.

17 Saturday

Sun conjunct Uranus is a time to embrace your authenticity, explore new possibilities, and step out of your comfort zone. Unexpected opportunities and sudden insights may arise, propelling you towards exciting new paths. Embrace the spirit of adventure and allow your true essence to shine brightly. Remember to balance your desire for freedom with mindful consideration of others as you navigate this dynamic and transformative energy.

18 Sunday

When Mercury squares Mars, it can bring a dynamic and potentially challenging energy to your communication and mental processes. You may be more assertive and direct in expressing your thoughts and ideas. However, your interactions can also tend to impatience, impulsiveness, and conflict. It's essential to be mindful of your words and actions during this time, as the square aspect can amplify the potential for misunderstandings and arguments.

19 Monday

New options crop up to inspire a sense of wanderlust. Reawakening creativity brings growth and happiness into your life. Your pioneering spirit lets you turn the corner and connect with expansion, adventure, and excitement. You soon hit your stride in a journey that grows your life in a unique direction. Listening to the call of the wild within your spirit heightens confidence and brings motivation to continue growing your life.

20 Tuesday

Your communication skills and intellectual curiosity are rising as the Sun enters Gemini. You may find yourself more friendly and inclined to engage in lively conversations. This aspect is an excellent time to expand your knowledge, share ideas, and connect with others through your words. Remember to balance your mental agility with a grounded approach, and use your communication skills to build bridges and foster understanding.

21 Wednesday

Changes swirling around your life help you dive toward new potential. You discover a unique vantage point that brings a broader overview of your life. Gaining insight into the path ahead brings new avenues of growth that offer more excellent stability in your life. It lights an enchanting way forward that sees creativity coursing through your choices and decisions. It brings a time of using your talents to forge an enterprising trail towards the development of dreams.

22 Thursday

Venus forms a harmonious trine aspect with Mars, bringing passion, harmony, and attraction. This aspect enhances your ability to assert yourself in a balanced and charming way, making it easier to pursue your desires and forge meaningful connections with others. It's a time to embrace your magnetism and confidently express your wishes. With the Sun forming a sextile aspect with Neptune, there is rising imagination, intuition, and spiritual awareness.

23 Friday

Opening the book to a new chapter brings a gateway forward. It nurtures your creativity and helps you build something substantial in your life. It teams you up with others who match your interests as you draw movement and discovery into your world. You enter an extensive phase of rising prospects that get the ball rolling on growing your life outwardly. Changing circumstances reinvigorate your life, and from these shifting foundations, you reach for a lofty goal.

24 Saturday

When the Sun forms a harmonious trine aspect with Pluto, it brings a powerful energy of transformation and personal growth into your life. It empowers you to delve deep into your subconscious, uncover hidden truths, and make profound changes in your life. You may experience a heightened sense of personal power and a greater understanding of your inner motivations and desires. With the Moon entering Taurus, you are grounded and focused on practical matters.

25 Sunday

When Saturn enters Aries, you may embark on a new chapter of discipline, structure, and responsibility. This transition prompts you to take a more proactive and assertive approach to achieving your goals and establishing a solid foundation. Saturn in Aries challenges you to confront and overcome obstacles with patience, determination, and perseverance. It's a time to set clear boundaries, prioritize self-discipline, and take calculated risks to pursue your ambitions.

26 Monday

As Mercury moves into Gemini, your communication and mental processes become more agile. This transit enhances your ability to express yourself clearly and engage in meaningful conversations. With Mercury forming a harmonious sextile with Saturn, your thoughts are focused, allowing you to make practical decisions and plans. The Moon's ingress into Gemini further enhances your mental agility, making it a time for studying and gathering information.

27 Tuesday

During the New Moon, a powerful cosmic portal opens up for you. It is a time of new beginnings and fresh possibilities. With Mercury forming a trine to Pluto, your thoughts and communication gain depth and intensity. This aspect enhances your ability to delve into the depths of your mind, uncover hidden truths, and engage in profound conversations. You may find yourself drawn to uncovering the mysteries of life and seeking transformational experiences.

28 Wednesday

Moon ingress Cancer is a favorable moment to create a nurturing space for yourself, engage in self-care activities, and cultivate a sense of emotional balance. Embrace the gentle waves of sensitivity and compassion that flow through you, and allow them to guide your actions and interactions with others. You can navigate this Moon in Cancer with grace and understanding by honoring your emotions and creating a harmonious environment.

29 Thursday

Life offers new possibilities that help you navigate greener pastures. Essentially, it enables you to create a bridge towards a brighter chapter. Good energy flows easily and naturally into your world as you reveal exciting options that offer a buzz of excitement. It underscores a time of change ahead in your life that helps things fall into place. Letting go of fixed expectations enables you to move beyond areas that limit progress.

JUNE

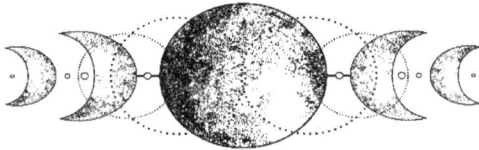

MOON MAGIC

Sun	Mon	Tue	Wed	Thu	Fri	Sat
1	2	3	4	5	6	7
8	9	10	11	12	13	14
15	16	17	18	19	20	21
22	23	24	25	26	27	28
29	30					

NEW MOON

_____

_____

_____

_____

_____

_____

_____

_____

_____

_____

_____

_____

_____

_____

_____

_____

_____

_____

_____

_____

_____

STRAWBERRY MOON

---

30 Friday

Sun conjunct Mercury. Moon ingress Leo. It's a time to embrace your inner spark and express yourself creatively through art, performance, or simply sharing your authentic self with others. Allow the synergy between the Sun, Mercury, and the Moon in Leo to inspire you to confidently express your truth, speak your mind, and enter the spotlight. Let your light shine brightly, and embrace the power of self-expression.

31 Saturday

You can improve life by being open to new possibilities as news arrives, which inspires change. It brings an upgrade that promotes more sunshine and happiness. The path ahead glimmers with refreshing potential. You get a glimpse of a compelling journey that offers a social aspect that feels like a good fit for your life. It opens your circle to new people and spotlights developing enriching bonds worth your time.

1 Sunday

Life becomes lighter and sweeter as you step away from drama and surround yourself with people who support your life. Changes in the air bring a busy aspect as news, invitations, and opportunities to mingle link you to a lively and dynamic time. Growing your social life brings constructive dialogues and opportunities to entertain with friends who enrich your life. It lets you blaze towards a self-expressive journey.

2 Monday

As the Moon moves into Virgo, you can focus on details and concentrate on practical matters. It is when you can bring a sense of organization and efficiency to your daily life. Pay attention to the little things and strive for precision in your tasks. Your analytical skills heighten, allowing you to solve problems and address challenges practically and precisely. Use this period to care for your physical well-being and engage in activities promoting health and self-care.

3 Tuesday

Experimenting with new pathways brings an upward trend that promotes advancement in your working life. It offers an uptick of potential that becomes a source of prosperity as you create progress in developing a meaningful goal in your life. A theme of improving circumstances cracks the code to a brighter chapter. You reap the rewards of new options, which open a path of change, growth, and success.

4 Wednesday

As the Moon moves into Libra, it heightens the sense of harmony and a desire for balance in your life. It is a time to create peace and unity in your relationships and surroundings. You may find yourself seeking compromises and finding common ground in conflicts. Your natural inclination towards diplomacy and fairness can help you navigate challenging situations gracefully and tactfully. It's an excellent time to engage in cooperative endeavors and collaborate.

5 Thursday

When Venus sextiles Jupiter, you can expect a harmonious and expansive energy in your relationships and experiences. This aspect brings joy, optimism, and abundance to your life. You may feel receptive to new opportunities in love, social connections, or creative endeavors. It's a time to embrace the beauty around you and indulge in the pleasures of life. Your communication skills enhance as Mercury sextiles Mars, allowing you to express confidence and assertiveness.

6 Friday

When Venus ingresses Taurus, it brings an energy shift that enhances your appreciation for beauty, comfort, and sensual pleasures. You may find yourself more attuned to the joys of the physical world and life's simple pleasures. This phase is a time to indulge in self-care, pamper yourself, and surround yourself with things that bring you joy. You may feel a greater need for stability and security in your relationships, seeking a sense of loyalty, commitment, and groundedness.

7 Saturday

When the Moon ingresses Scorpio, it brings an intense and transformative energy to your emotional landscape. You may find yourself diving deep into your feelings and exploring the hidden depths of your psyche. This transit is a time for introspection and self-discovery as you uncover layers of emotions buried beneath the surface. You are encouraged to embrace your emotional truth and allow yourself to be vulnerable.

8 Sunday

When Mercury conjuncts Jupiter and ingress into Cancer, you may feel a surge of intellectual expansion and deepening emotional understanding. Your mind becomes receptive to new ideas and perspectives, and you can see the bigger picture. Your communication style becomes more compassionate and empathetic, allowing you to connect deeply with others. It is when you can express your thoughts and feelings with greater sensitivity and understanding.

9 Monday

Venus square Pluto can bring intensity and power dynamics into your relationships and personal values. Navigating these dynamics with awareness and honesty is essential, as they can prompt transformation and growth. With Jupiter's ingress into Cancer, you may feel nurturing energy. This transit is a time to focus on home, family, and emotional well-being. Trust your intuition and allow yourself to follow your heart in navigating these cosmic energies.

10 Tuesday

The current astrological configuration signals a surge of cosmic energy that propels you forward. It's a universal push to embrace challenges and pursue your ambitions with renewed vigor. Feel the dynamism in the air, and trust that the universe is aligning to support your endeavors. As life picks up steam, a more productive pace sees potential blossoming in your world. It lets you come up with a winning journey that offers transformation.

11 Wednesday

During the Full Moon, you may experience heightened emotions and awareness. It's a time of illumination and culmination, where the energy is potent and emotions are at their peak. This Full Moon brings the harmonious aspect of Mercury's sextile Venus, which enhances your communication and social interactions. It's a good time for expressing your thoughts and feelings with grace and charm, allowing for harmonious connections and meaningful conversations.

12 Thursday

The energy of Capricorn encourages you to take a grounded and organized approach to your emotions, allowing you to make progress and achieve stability. Use this time to assess your priorities, set realistic boundaries, and work towards your ambitions. You may feel a sense of determination and a willingness to put in the necessary effort to achieve your desired outcomes. The Capricorn energy guides you towards self-discipline, resilience, and gracefully handling challenges.

13 Friday

The cosmos pulses with heightened energy, sparking a vibrant atmosphere for social connections. Your social sphere becomes a source of encouragement and inspiration. Embrace this lively backdrop to cultivate new friendships and expand your circle. Sharing time with like-minded individuals lays the foundation for growth and joy, setting the stage for positive developments. It helps you touch down on a supportive and engaging journey you can cherish.

14 Saturday

The Moon in Aquarius encourages you to break free from traditional norms and embrace individuality. It's a time to express yourself and engage in activities that inspire your intellect and curiosity. Embrace the energy of Aquarius by embracing your inner rebel, thinking outside the box, and being open to new perspectives. You can cultivate your eccentricity and cherish the freedom to be authentic. Allow your emotions to flow freely and explore the possibilities during this period.

15 Sunday

When Mars squares Uranus and Jupiter squares Saturn, you may experience tension and challenge. Mars square Uranus can bring unexpected disruptions and sudden changes that require flexibility and adaptability. It's essential to exercise caution and think before taking impulsive actions during this time. Jupiter square Saturn creates a conflict between expansion and restriction, where you may feel limitation or frustration in pursuing your goals.

16 Monday

When the Moon enters Pisces, you may immerse yourself in a world of dreams, intuition, and emotional sensitivity. Your emotions become deeply attuned to the subtle energies around you, and you may feel greater empathy and compassion toward others. This transit is a time to honor your intuitive guidance and pay attention to your dreams and inner voice. Allow yourself to explore the depths of your emotions and connect with your spiritual side.

17 Tuesday

When Mars ingresses Virgo, you may find a boost of practicality and attention to detail entering your life. Virgo is an earth sign known for its meticulous nature and analytical approach. During this time, you are motivated to tackle tasks efficiently and precisely. Your focus shifts towards organization, productivity, and refining your skills. This transit is an excellent opportunity to establish healthy routines, set goals, and prioritize responsibilities.

18 Wednesday

When the Moon ingresses Aries, you may feel a surge of energy and a strong sense of motivation. You may feel a strong desire for independence and freedom and a willingness to take risks. Trust your instincts and follow your gut as you navigate this energetic and dynamic period. Embrace the opportunities for self-expression, adventure, and personal development that come your way. Let your inner fire ignite your passions and propel you on your chosen path.

19 Thursday

Jupiter square Neptune. Seek clarity and discernment in your endeavors, and be willing to make adjustments or reevaluate your plans as needed. This aspect calls for a balanced approach, where you can blend your dreams and aspirations with a practical understanding of potential limitations and challenges. This aspect can bring uncertainty regarding your beliefs and aspirations. Trust your intuition, stay adaptable, and find creative ways to navigate this dynamic energy.

20 Friday

As celestial energies unfold, relationships take center stage with an unpredictable flair. Be open to surprises in matters of the heart and expect the unexpected. This period encourages you to explore new facets of emotional connection, injecting an element of excitement and spontaneity into your interactions. Events align to form a favorable window of opportunity that shines a light on expanding your circle of friends.

21 Saturday

As the Moon moves into Taurus and the Sun enters Cancer during the June Solstice, you can embrace a nurturing and grounded energy. This cosmic alignment encourages you to focus on the stability and comfort of your surroundings. It's a time to reconnect with the pleasures of life and find solace in the simple joys that bring you a sense of security. Take this opportunity to honor your emotions and prioritize self-care.

22 Sunday

Mars sextile Jupiter. Sun square Saturn. By balancing the fiery energy of Mars and Jupiter with the structured power of Sun-Saturn, you can navigate this period with resilience, determination, and strategic planning. Stay focused on your long-term objectives and remain flexible, adapting to necessary changes. Your commitment and perseverance will ultimately lead to success and personal growth. These aspects encourage you to embrace opportunities for development and success.

23 Monday

Moon ingress Gemini. Sun square Neptune. By staying grounded and using your discernment, you can navigate through any illusions or distractions, allowing the positive energy of the Moon in Gemini to inspire curiosity, learning, and effective communication. Embrace the opportunity to explore new ideas and connect with others through open-minded conversations while remaining anchored in your truth and maintaining clarity amidst the Neptunian fog.

24 Tuesday

When the Sun aligns with Jupiter in conjunction, it signifies a time of expanded possibilities and abundant energy. This celestial union brings a sense of optimism and confidence to your life. You feel inspired to take on new challenges, explore uncharted territories, and embrace growth opportunities. The Sun's radiant energy merges with Jupiter's expansive influence, amplifying your enthusiasm and opening doors to new avenues of success.

25 Wednesday

The New Moon in Cancer encourages you to honor your emotions, listen to your intuition, and embrace vulnerability as you embark on a new chapter of your life. Take this time to reflect on your deepest desires and set intentions that align with your heart's most authentic wishes. By harnessing the transformative energy of the New Moon in Cancer, you can create a solid foundation for emotional well-being and set the stage for personal growth and fulfillment.

26 Thursday

Allow your mind to be open to new possibilities and embrace the spirit of adventure. With the Sun's sextile to Mars, you are infused with vitality and determination, enabling you to take action and pursue your goals enthusiastically. It's a favorable time to assert yourself and make progress in areas that are important to you. Trust your abilities and let your inner spark shine as you navigate this dynamic and intellectually stimulating period.

27 Friday

The Moon transitioning into Leo infuses you with radiant and expressive energy. This celestial shift invites you to embrace your unique qualities and let your inner light shine brightly. The Leo Moon encourages you to tap into your creativity, passion, and self-confidence. It's a time to embrace self-expression and let your authentic self be seen and heard. Allow yourself to take center stage and share your talents and gifts with the world.

28 Saturday

Mercury trine Saturn alignment empowers you to think strategically, make sound decisions, and confidently plan for the future. Your ability to concentrate and absorb information is enhanced, allowing you to dive deep into complex subjects and find practical solutions. At the same time, Neptune's influence brings inspiration and intuition to your thoughts and words. You have a heightened sensitivity to subtle energies and a deep understanding of the unseen realms.

29 Sunday

Mercury-opposed Pluto alignment encourages you to be discerning and critical in your thinking, allowing you to uncover hidden insights and make necessary adjustments. While the opposition may bring some internal tension, the Virgo influence helps you channel this energy into productive and constructive actions. Focus on finding the balance between your emotions and rationality, and use this time to refine your ideas and plans for greater effectiveness and efficiency.

JULY

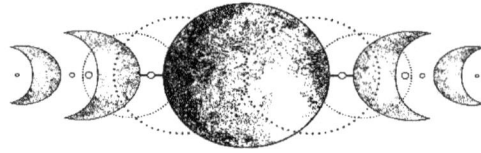

MOON MAGIC

Sun	Mon	Tue	Wed	Thu	Fri	Sat
		1	2	3	4	5
6	7	8	9	10	11	12
13	14	15	16	17	18	19
20	21	22	23	24	25	26
27	28	29	30	31		

LIBRA

New Moon

BUCK MOON

30 Monday

Haumea, the cosmic nurturer, showers your life with fertility and abundance. During this period, cultivate the celestial soil of your ambitions. Just as Haumea nurtures life, let your endeavors blossom and flourish, bearing the fruits of your cosmic labor. Like a cosmic architect, this time invites you to rebuild the structures of your life. Embrace the cosmic tools at your disposal, turning challenges into stepping stones on your journey of personal and spiritual renewal.

1 Tuesday

When the Moon enters Libra, you may seek balance and harmony in your emotional and social interactions. Your focus shifts towards creating and maintaining harmonious relationships with others. You are naturally inclined to consider different perspectives and find common ground, which can lead to more peaceful and cooperative interactions. You may desire companionship and social connection, valuing the support and understanding of your relationships.

2 Wednesday

As the celestial energies align, the archetype of Atlas beckons you to embody cosmic endurance. Picture yourself standing firm; shoulders squared against the trials of the universe. This period urges you not merely to withstand challenges but to thrive under their weight. Embrace the endurance of Atlas, and let the burdens you carry sculpt the strength that defines you. Your cosmic grit will be the cornerstone of achievements yet to unfold.

3 Thursday

Like a centaur galloping through the cosmic expanse, this period calls for a spirited exploration of mind, body, and spirit. Embrace the wild and untamed aspects of your being. Allow the cosmic centaur's energy to guide you on a transformative journey of self-discovery and holistic growth. This period invites you to cultivate the sacred flame within, nurturing your passions and dedicating yourself to pursuits that ignite your soul with cosmic purpose.

4 Friday

When the Moon enters Scorpio, you may experience a deepening of emotions and a heightened sense of intensity. This astrological transit invites you to delve into the depths of your psyche and explore your inner world. It's a time for introspection and introspection, where you may feel more attuned to your desires, passions, and hidden truths. With Venus conjunct Uranus, there is a sense of excitement and unpredictability in your relationships and personal values.

5 Saturday

Eris, the celestial provocateur, stirs cosmic discord to awaken dormant aspects of your consciousness. Embrace the challenges that disrupt the status quo, for within chaos lies the potential for profound transformation. This period prompts you to confront discordant energies, fostering a deeper understanding of the cosmic dance between order and chaos. This period invites you to don the armor of insight and navigate the intricate tapestry of your journey with strategic finesse.

6 Sunday

With the Moon entering Sagittarius, you may feel a strong urge for adventure, exploration, and expanding your horizons. It's a time to embrace new experiences, broaden your knowledge, and seek a higher understanding of the world around you. Your enthusiasm and optimism shine through, motivating you to pursue your goals with passion and curiosity. Trust your inner guidance as you embark on this journey of discovery, and embrace the opportunities that come your way.

7 Monday

When Uranus enters Gemini, it brings dynamic and innovative energy to your communication and mental processes. This transit encourages you to embrace change, think outside the box, and explore new ideas. It sparks intellectual curiosity and stimulates your desire for academic freedom and unconventional thinking. As Venus forms a trine with Pluto, there is a deepening of your relationships and a transformative quality to your interactions.

8 Tuesday

Vesta, the guardian of cosmic dedication, illuminates your path with the sacred flame of commitment. This period calls for a deepened focus on your purpose. Allow Vesta's energy to fuel the fires of dedication, guiding you toward a life aligned with your celestial calling. This period prompts you to adopt a strategic approach to your cosmic endeavors. Channel Vestas' energy as you navigate the cosmic chessboard, making mindful moves that lead to success and fulfillment.

9 Wednesday

With the Moon entering Capricorn, you may be in a more focused and disciplined state of mind. This lunar transit encourages you to channel your energy toward practical matters and long-term goals. It's a time for setting intentions, creating structure, and taking a responsible approach to your endeavors. You may feel a more substantial need for stability and achievement and a desire to be productive and progress in your professional or personal life.

10 Thursday

The Full Moon is a potent time for reflection, culmination, and release. It invites you to examine various aspects of your life and assess your progress. You may feel a surge of emotions and need closure or resolution. It's an opportune moment to let go of what no longer serves you and embrace a sense of renewal. The Full Moon illuminates areas that require your attention, allowing you to gain clarity and make necessary adjustments.

11 Friday

When the Moon enters Aquarius, you may feel a sense of freedom and independence. This cosmic alignment is when your focus shifts towards broader perspectives and social connections. You may feel more inclined to seek like-minded individuals and engage in intellectually stimulating conversations. As you tap into your inner vision, your innovative and unique ideas may flow more easily during this period.

12 Saturday

Ceres, the cosmic harvester, invites you to reap the rewards of your cosmic efforts. This period marks a time of abundance and fulfillment. Just as Ceres gathers the astral harvest, relish in the bountiful fruits of your labor, recognizing the cosmic cycles of sowing and reaping. This period calls for a harmonious dance with the cosmic forces that surround you. Tune into Cere's heavenly music, finding grace and joy in the dance of existence.

13 Sunday

When Saturn turns retrograde, it signals a time of introspection and reflection in your life. You may feel a sense of slowing down and turning inward as you assess your goals, responsibilities, and structures. This transit allows you to review and revise your long-term plans, ensuring they align with your values and aspirations. The Moon's ingress into Pisces adds a touch of sensitivity and intuition to this introspective period.

14 Monday

You are amidst a transformation that brings new options into your life. Your efforts to improve circumstances bear fruit and offer rising security. News ahead lights an exciting path forward for your working life. It gives you the green light to get involved with an endeavor that opens a fortunate trend for your career path. Setting your sights on achieving growth brings a time of progress and advancement. Life heads to an upswing as a prosperous cycle emerges.

15 Tuesday

An emphasis on improving your situation draws an inspiring journey into your life. Rising prospects ahead crack the code to expand life outwardly. You discover a new approach that draws momentum into your world, and as the pace of life quickens, you soon feel buoyed by encouraging results. Being proactive helps you gain a foothold in an ambitious and exciting area. It places you on a path of growth and advancement.

16 Wednesday

Moon ingress Aries. Trust your instincts and take bold steps forward. You have the courage and determination to overcome obstacles and achieve success. Use this dynamic energy to ignite your passions and pursue your dreams. Take charge of your life and embrace the spirit of adventure. It's a time of self-discovery and embracing your individuality. Embrace the fire within you and let it fuel your personal growth and fulfillment journey.

17 Thursday

The cosmic mirror of Selene casts a luminous glow upon your inner waters, inviting you to navigate the currents of introspection. Dive into the reflective depths, for within them lie the secrets of your emotional landscape. Allow Selene's cosmic reflection to illuminate the recesses of your soul, revealing hidden facets that, once acknowledged, contribute to the mosaic of your true self. Embrace the heavenly radiance, for it is in this luminosity that shadows dissipate.

18 Friday

When Mercury turns retrograde, you might notice a shift in your communication and thought processes. It's a time to slow down, reflect, and review your plans and ideas. As the Moon enters Taurus, you may feel a grounding influence that encourages practicality and stability. This combination of energies allows you to approach situations calmly and patiently. The sextile between Mercury and Venus enhances your ability to express yourself with charm and diplomacy.

19 Saturday

Haumea, the celestial midwife, presides over periods of gestation and rebirth. This cosmic phase encourages you to embrace the fertile space of transformation. Just as Haumea oversees the birth of new celestial bodies, this period prompts you to nurture the seeds of change within, allowing them to blossom into cosmic expressions of your evolving self. Embrace the growth, for in the cosmic energies, there lies the potential for profound personal evolution.

20 Sunday

Moon ingress Gemini. Embrace the versatile nature of Gemini and allow yourself to be flexible and adaptable in your approach. Seek out intellectual stimulation and engage in activities that challenge your mind. It is a period of heightened communication, so express yourself freely and connect with others through meaningful conversations. Embrace the curious spirit of Gemini and embrace the opportunities for growth and expansion that come your way.

21 Monday

You benefit from this dynamic chapter as it offers a productive environment that cultivates pleasing results. Exploring new pathways illuminates exciting changes ahead. It brings visionary ideas that open your life outwardly. With strategic prowess, envision your cosmic chessboard, each move executed with precision and foresight, ensuring that your journey unfolds according to the heavenly plans you've set in motion.

22 Tuesday

When the Moon moves into Cancer and the Sun enters Leo, you may feel a shift in your emotional and creative energy. Cancer's nurturing and sensitivity encourage you to prioritize self-care and emotional well-being. It's a time to listen to your intuition and honor your emotions. You may find comfort in creating a safe and cozy environment where you can retreat and recharge. Meanwhile, the Sun in Leo adds a touch of confidence and self-expression to your life.

23 Wednesday

As the Sun forms a sextile with Uranus and Venus squares Mars, you can explore new possibilities and embrace individuality. The Sun's harmonious aspect with Uranus sparks excitement and opens doors to innovative ideas and opportunities. It encourages you to step out of your comfort zone, embrace change, and express your unique self. Meanwhile, Venus square Mars creates a dynamic tension between your desires and relationships.

24 Thursday

With the Sun trine Saturn, you have a fantastic opportunity to harness your inner strength and perseverance. This aspect brings stability, discipline, and a strong sense of responsibility to your endeavors. It's a time to set clear goals, establish solid foundations, and work diligently towards your ambitions. As the Moon ingresses Leo, you infuse with confidence, creativity, and self-expression. You feel inspired to shine your light and embrace your unique talents and abilities.

25 Friday

When the Sun opposes Pluto, you may experience power struggles and transformative dynamics in various areas of your life. This aspect creates a clash between your ego and the forces of change and transformation. It challenges you to confront your deepest fears, face hidden truths, and let go of old patterns that no longer serve you. It is a time of profound self-discovery and growth as you navigate the depths of your psyche and confront the shadows within.

26 Saturday

Moon ingress Virgo is when you pay attention to the details, analyze situations, and focus on practical matters. Your inner world becomes more grounded and focused as you seek efficiency and effectiveness in your daily routines. You may find satisfaction in organizing your environment, attending to tasks, and seeking a sense of order and cleanliness. This lunar transit encourages you to be diligent, reliable, and attentive to the small details contributing to your overall well-being.

27 Sunday

Orcus, the celestial transformer, stands as a guardian of profound change. This period prompts you to embrace the cosmic alchemy of transformation. Like a phoenix rising from the ashes, allow Orcus' energy to guide you through the cosmic cycles of death and rebirth, emerging stronger and wiser. Embrace and let your creative instincts flow. In doing so, you discover the birthplace of cosmic innovation and artistic expression.

28 Monday

Exploring options in your life triggers a new path that shines a light on advancement. It helps you turn a corner and grow your talents as you extend your reach into developing an intrepid trail worth your time. Your sense of optimism is a golden key that opens new possibilities for your life. Stirring the essence of manifestation lifts the lid on growing your life outwardly. It brings a busy time that offers up trailblazing options.

29 Tuesday

With the Moon moving into Libra, you may experience a shift towards harmony, balance, and a desire for connection in your emotional landscape. During this transit, you might find yourself more attuned to the needs and feelings of others, seeking to foster understanding and cooperation in your relationships. Social interactions and partnerships could hold greater significance, and you might seek out shared activities and experiences.

30 Wednesday

Astraea, the cosmic goddess of justice, stands as a beacon in the celestial court, calling for cosmic fairness and equilibrium. Envision yourself holding the scales of justice, carefully weighing your actions and decisions. This period is an opportunity to align with cosmic justice, ensuring that your journey is characterized by integrity, fairness, and a sense of moral equilibrium. This period encourages you to cultivate harmony within and without.

31 Thursday

The cosmic rebel, Ixion, extends an invitation to liberate yourself from self-imposed constraints. Picture breaking free from the chains that bind your spirit. This period is a cosmic rebellion against limitations, a call to embrace the freedom to express your authentic self. Release the shackles that hinder your cosmic journey and allow Ixion's liberating energy to propel you toward uncharted realms of possibility.

AUGUST

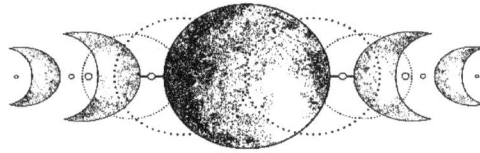

MOON MAGIC

Sun	Mon	Tue	Wed	Thu	Fri	Sat
					1	2
3	4	5	6	7	8	9
10	11	12	13	14	15	16
17	18	19	20	21	22	23
24	25	26	27	28	29	30
31						

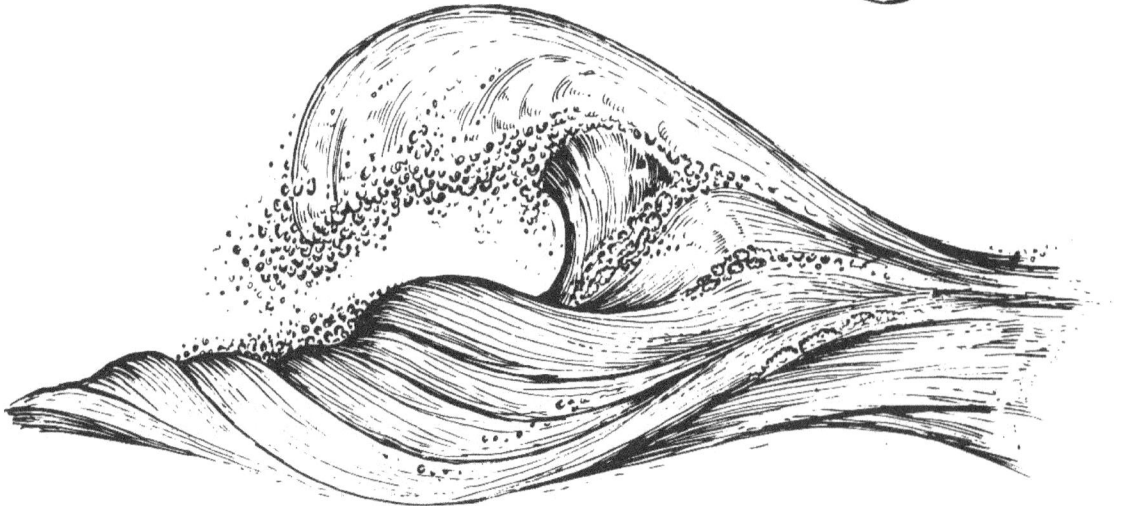

New Moon

STURGEON MOON

1 Friday

With Venus forming challenging squares with Saturn and Neptune, you might experience tension and confusion in your relationships and personal desires. Saturn's influence may bring about feelings of restriction and limitation, making it difficult to express affection and receive love from others. You could feel a sense of detachment or distance in your connections, leading to a need for patience and perseverance.

2 Saturday

Huya, the cosmic revealer, unveils hidden truths and cosmic mysteries. This period encourages you to seek the deeper meanings behind life's experiences. Embrace the heavenly revelations, allowing Huya's energy to guide you toward a greater understanding of your place in the vast cosmic tapestry. This period invites you to seek enlightenment and awareness. Allow Huya's radiant energy to illuminate your path, revealing the wisdom that resides within and around you.

3 Sunday

When the Moon enters Sagittarius, you may feel enthusiasm and optimism. This placement encourages you to seek new adventures and broaden your horizons. You might strongly desire freedom and exploration, wanting to break free from any restrictions or limitations. It's a great time to engage in activities stimulating your mind and spirit, such as travel, learning, or connecting with people from different backgrounds.

4 Monday

Exploring options generates new leads that offer rising prospects. It lets you chart a course toward improving your situation as you open a highly productive cycle that brings new possibilities into your life. It opens the floodgates to lighter energy, which marks a turning point as you build growth around your life. Picture the gate swinging open, revealing pathways of cosmic potential and beckoning you toward the cosmic adventures that await.

5 Tuesday

Moon ingress Capricorn is a time to take a disciplined and structured approach to your emotions and to be mindful of any self-imposed limitations or fears that may hold you back. Use the Moon in Capricorn to build a solid foundation for your feelings and to take practical steps towards manifesting your dreams. Take advantage of this time to be ambitious, determined, and focused on your emotional growth and success.

6 Wednesday

As Mars enters Libra, you may seek more harmony and balance in your actions and relationships. This transit encourages you to approach conflicts with a diplomatic and cooperative attitude. You may feel compelled to work on improving partnerships and seeking win-win solutions in your interactions with others. It's a time to find compromises and seek common ground rather than engage in confrontations.

7 Thursday

Picture Asteria, the cosmic Dreamweaver, extending her cosmic loom before you. This period encourages you to dream expansively and set cosmic aspirations. Envision your dreams taking shape in the vast cosmic tapestry, each thread woven into the fabric of your reality. Let Asteria's heavenly dreams guide you as you embark on a journey where the boundless realms of your imagination converge with the infinite possibilities of the cosmos.

8 Friday

With the Moon moving into Aquarius and forming a trine with Uranus, you may experience a surge of unique and innovative energy. This alignment encourages you to embrace your individuality and explore new and unconventional ways of approaching challenges. You might find yourself inspired to break free from routine and seek out exciting adventures or opportunities for personal growth. It is a favorable time to take risks, try new things, and embrace change.

9 Saturday

With Mars opposing Saturn and Neptune during this Full Moon, you might feel a sense of tension and conflicting energies. Mars represents your drive and assertiveness, while Saturn and Neptune bring in themes of restriction and illusion. It could lead to frustration and feeling pulled in different directions. You may find it challenging to progress your goals, and self-doubt could creep in. It's essential to be mindful of any impulsive actions or rash decisions during this time.

10 Sunday

The Moon in Pisces enhances your intuitive and compassionate nature, encouraging you to connect with your inner self and understand the deeper aspects of your emotions. It's a favorable time for introspection and creative pursuits. Meanwhile, the harmonious trine between Mars and Pluto empowers you to take confident action and make meaningful changes. You feel a sense of determination and the ability to overcome obstacles holding you back.

11 Monday

With Mercury turning direct, you may feel a sense of relief and clarity after a period of introspection and reassessment. Communication and decision-making are likely to become smoother and more straightforward now. It's an excellent time to tie up loose ends, finalize plans, and move forward with any projects on hold during the retrograde phase. You might notice a greater flow of information and ideas, making it easier to express and share your thoughts with others.

12 Tuesday

With Saturn sextile Uranus, you may find a harmonious balance between tradition and innovation. This aspect encourages you to embrace change while still honoring the lessons and structures of the past. It's a great time to progress steadily toward your goals while being open to new and exciting opportunities. Alongside this, the Venus conjunct Jupiter aspect brings optimism, joy, and abundance to your relationships and experiences.

13 Wednesday

Helios, the cosmic sun, showers your life with radiant energy. This period marks a time of illumination and clarity. Bask in the celestial radiance of Helios, allowing the light to dispel shadows and brighten the pathways of your journey. This period encourages you to seek cosmic justice in your interactions and relationships. Channel Helio's energy as you navigate the scales of balance, ensuring that your cosmic actions are aligned with integrity and fairness.

14 Thursday

With the Moon's ingress into Taurus, you might notice a calming and grounding influence on your emotions and approach to life. This shift can bring a sense of stability and comfort, encouraging you to savor the simple pleasures and find contentment in the present moment. You may feel drawn to activities that provide security and nourishment, such as enjoying good food, spending time in nature, or creating a cozy and peaceful atmosphere at home.

AUGUST

15 Friday

With Mercury sextile Mars, you may notice increased mental sharpness and assertiveness. This aspect can boost your communication skills and make expressing yourself confidently and assertively easier. Your thoughts and ideas may flow more smoothly, and you may find it easier to take action on your plans and projects. It's a favorable time for making decisions, initiating conversations, and tackling tasks that require quick thinking and decisiveness.

16 Saturday

With the Moon's ingress into Gemini, you might feel a noticeable shift in your emotions and focus. Your curiosity and mental agility increase, leading you to seek new information and experiences. You may feel more friendly and eager to engage in conversations with others. It is an excellent time for networking, learning, and exploring diverse topics. Your mind is adaptable and open to different perspectives, which is great for problem-solving and creative thinking.

17 Sunday

Thalassa, the cosmic flow, guides you through the ebb and flow of life's currents. This period encourages you to surrender to the cosmic tides, trusting in the natural rhythms of existence. Embrace Thalassa's energy, allowing the cosmic currents to carry you toward new shores of experience and growth. Embrace Thalassa's power as a source of cosmic medicine, allowing any old wounds to transform into sources of wisdom and strength.

18 Monday

When Mercury forms a sextile with Mars, you may experience a boost in your communication and mental agility. Your thoughts become sharper, and you find it easier to articulate your ideas with confidence and assertiveness. Simultaneously, the Moon's ingress into Cancer heightens your emotional sensitivity and nurtures a profound connection to your inner self. This combination fuels passions, encouraging decisive actions to pursue your goals.

19 Tuesday

Channel the wisdom of Metis, the cosmic counselor. Picture this period as a cosmic consultation, with Metis guiding you through the labyrinth of choices and challenges. Envision tapping into the cosmic well of knowledge, drawing on the perceptive insights that ensure your decisions are steeped in wisdom and foresight. Envision this period as a cosmic workshop where your ideas, like celestial sparks, have the potential to set ablaze new trails of creativity and transformative energy.

20 Wednesday

As the Moon transitions into Leo, you may notice a shift in your emotional landscape. This celestial event brings vibrant and expressive energy into your life, igniting your passion and creativity. You might seek attention and recognition, and your emotions could be more dramatic and pronounced. It's a time to embrace your inner fire, allowing your authentic self to shine. Enjoy the spotlight, and let your individuality take the stage for an exciting and fulfilling lunar transition.

21 Thursday

Embody the victorious spirit of Heracles as celestial energies align in your favor. Picture this period as a cosmic coliseum, where you emerge triumphant from the battles you've faced. Envision the laurel wreaths of cosmic victory adorning your cosmic brow, a symbol of your resilience and the cosmic conquests that await you on the horizon. Designing your life draws progression and aligns you towards achieving a positive result.

22 Friday

As the Sun enters Virgo, you may feel a shift in focus toward organization, practicality, and attention to detail. This transit encourages you to analyze and assess your goals clearly and discerningly. You might find yourself drawn to refining your daily routines and seeking ways to improve efficiency in various aspects of your life. It is an excellent time to prioritize self-care and well-being, as the Virgo influence promotes healthy habits and a disciplined approach to life.

23 Saturday

With the Moon's ingress into Virgo and the arrival of the New Moon, a period of introspection and practical planning lies ahead for you. Pay attention to the details and approach matters with a methodical mindset. You may desire to analyze your emotions and thoughts, seeking ways to improve and bring order to your life. The New Moon offers a fresh start, making it an opportune moment to set intentions and goals that align with Virgo's qualities of organization and self-improvement.

24 Sunday

As the Sun forms a square with Uranus, you may experience unpredictability and a desire for freedom and change. This cosmic alignment can bring sudden shifts and disruptions, challenging you to break free from routine and embrace innovation. You might feel a strong urge to rebel against constraints and seek independence in various aspects. While this energy can be exhilarating, it's essential to be mindful of impulsive decisions with long-term consequences.

25 Monday

The Moon in Libra encourages you to seek balance and harmony in your interactions, fostering a diplomatic and fair-minded approach to dealing with others. Your desire for companionship and cooperation heightens during this transit. With Venus gracing Leo, your affections become more vibrant and theatrical, and you may feel a more substantial need for appreciation and admiration from those around you.

26 Tuesday

The trine to Neptune fosters a dreamy and compassionate atmosphere, encouraging acts of kindness and empathy towards others. You may find inspiration in artistic or spiritual endeavors during this period, deepening your emotional connection to the world around you. Embrace the harmonious energy of these aspects to foster genuine relationships and enrich your life with love, passion, and creativity.

27 Wednesday

You may encounter intense emotional experiences and power struggles with Venus opposing Pluto. This astrological aspect can bring jealousy, possessiveness, and a desire to control or manipulate situations. It's essential to be aware of any hidden agendas or obsessions that might arise during this time. Be mindful of handling conflicts and confrontations with loved ones as the potential for emotional volatility heightens.

28 Thursday

As the Moon enters Scorpio, you might notice a shift in your emotions and a desire to delve into more profound, more intense experiences. Scorpio's influence brings a sense of passion and determination to your feelings, making you more inclined to seek out hidden truths and uncover underlying motivations. During this time, you may feel more introspective and drawn to introspection, allowing you to understand your emotions profoundly.

29 Friday

With Uranus forming a sextile aspect to Neptune, you may experience a period of heightened creativity and spiritual insight. This celestial alignment encourages you to explore innovative ideas and unconventional approaches in various aspects of your life. Your intuition and imagination enhance, opening doors to new possibilities and a deeper understanding of metaphysical realms. Trust your instinct and allow it to guide clarity and a profound connection with the world.

30 Saturday

As the Moon enters Sagittarius, you may feel a sense of adventurousness and optimism permeate your emotions. This lunar transit encourages you to embrace a more expansive and open-minded approach to life. You may seek new experiences, knowledge, and wisdom that broaden your horizons and challenge your perspectives. Sagittarius' influence inspires a sense of wanderlust and a desire for freedom, prompting you to explore different cultures, philosophies, or beliefs.

31 Sunday

The cosmic archetype of love and desire, Eros, ignites the flames of passion within your celestial sphere. Envision a celebration of love in its myriad forms—passionate, creative, and transformative. During this period, allow Eros' energy to infuse your pursuits with fervor, deepening your connections with others and kindling the creative fires that propel you forward. You launch towards an enriching environment filled with lively conversations.

SEPTEMBER

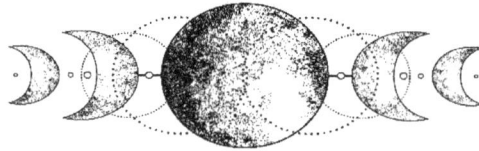

MOON MAGIC

Sun	Mon	Tue	Wed	Thu	Fri	Sat
	1	2	3	4	5	6
7	8	9	10	11	12	13
14	15	16	17	18	19	20
21	22	23	24	25	26	27
28	29	30				

NEW MOON

Corn/Harvest Moon

SEPTEMBER

1 Monday

Saturn's presence in Pisces invites you to establish firm yet flexible boundaries, allowing you to balance your dreams and aspirations with the practical aspects of life. Staying grounded and avoiding getting lost in fantasy or escapism is essential during this transition. Embrace the lessons of Saturn in Pisces as an opportunity for emotional growth and a deeper connection to your inner self. Embracing emotional maturity allows you to navigate this path with wisdom and sensitivity.

2 Tuesday

The Capricorn Moon instills a sense of responsibility and ambition, urging you to focus on your long-term goals and take calculated steps toward achieving them. This transit is a favorable time to organize your thoughts and express yourself with clarity and precision, as Mercury in Virgo enhances your analytical and critical thinking abilities. You may find satisfaction in attending to details and solving problems with practical solutions.

3 Wednesday

With Mercury forming a square aspect to Uranus, you may experience a period of mental restlessness and unconventional thinking. Your thoughts and ideas could be erratic and rebellious, making it challenging to focus on routine tasks. This astrological influence can bring sudden insights and breakthroughs but may also lead to impulsive decisions and communication mishaps. It's essential to be open to new perspectives but avoid hasty conclusions.

4 Thursday

As the Moon enters Aquarius, you may notice a shift in your emotional landscape, fostering a sense of open-mindedness and a desire for unique experiences. Aquarius' influence encourages you to embrace your individuality and be more accepting of others' differences. During this lunar transition, you might feel drawn to social causes and group activities, seeking a sense of belonging and connection within your community.

5 Friday

With Mars forming a square aspect to Jupiter, you might experience a surge of energy and enthusiasm. Still, it's essential to be mindful of potential excesses and impulsivity during this astrological influence. The square can create a sense of restlessness and a desire to take on too much at once, which could lead to overextending yourself or biting off more than you can chew. While enthusiasm can be invigorating, it's crucial to channel it wisely and avoid rash actions.

6 Saturday

You might find yourself more attuned to the feelings of others and drawn to creative or spiritual pursuits. During this period, allow yourself to explore the depths of your imagination and dive into the world of dreams. Embrace Uranus's retrograde energy and the Pisces Moon's ethereal influence to find inspiration, compassion, and a profound connection to your inner self. Use this time to make internal shifts, eventually leading to positive changes in your external world.

7 Sunday

Full Moon. This lunar phase encourages you to release anything that no longer serves you, whether it's emotional baggage, outdated beliefs, or unproductive habits. As the Full Moon shines its light on your life, it's an opportunity to gain clarity, find closure, and set new intentions moving forward. You might express yourself authentically and communicate your needs and desires. Embrace this powerful lunar energy to catalyze personal growth and positive transformation.

8 Monday

As the Moon enters Aries, you may feel a surge of energy and assertiveness. Aries' influence brings a sense of enthusiasm and courage, encouraging you to take initiative and pursue your goals with determination. This lunar transit can ignite your passion and drive, making it a favorable time to start new projects or assert your needs in various situations. Your emotions may be more spontaneous and direct, allowing you to express yourself authentically and boldly.

9 Tuesday

Embark on a Neptunian voyage across the cosmic sea of dreams. Picture your aspirations as celestial vessels sailing through the ethereal waves of inspiration. Envision yourself as the astral captain, steering your dreams toward uncharted celestial horizons. As you navigate this Neptunian realm, let the cosmic winds of imagination fill your sails, propelling you toward the realization of your most enchanting dreams.

10 Wednesday

As the Moon enters Taurus, you may experience a shift towards a more grounded and stable emotional state. Taurus' influence brings a sense of calm and practicality to your feelings, encouraging you to seek comfort and security in your surroundings. During this lunar transit, you might enjoy simple and sensory aspects, such as indulging in delicious food, spending time in nature, or enjoying soothing activities.

11 Thursday

Step into the cosmic ballroom and join the celestial dance of fate. Picture each step as a cosmic alignment, guiding you through the celestial waltz of chance and fortune. Envision yourself twirling through the cosmic rhythms, gracefully navigating the dance floor of destiny. In this celestial ballroom, serendipity becomes your dance partner, leading you through the choreography of unexpected joys and cosmic encounters.

12 Friday

With Mercury forming a sextile to Jupiter, your thoughts and communication skills are rising, making it an ideal time to express your ideas enthusiastically and persuasively. Embrace this positive and intellectually stimulating energy to seek new experiences, broaden your horizons, and make the most of the opportunities that come your way. This period encourages you to embrace a can-do attitude and trust your abilities to achieve your goals and manifest your aspirations.

13 Saturday

Sun conjunct Mercury. It's a favorable time for engaging in conversations, sharing your opinions, and making presentations, as your words carry a sense of authority and authenticity. This conjunction also boosts your intellectual capacity, allowing you to absorb information more readily and from a broader perspective. Embrace the powerful synergy of the Sun and Mercury to embrace opportunities for learning, self-expression, and making your voice heard with impact and influence.

14 Sunday

Envision the intricate threads of connection, weaving a cosmic tapestry that binds you to the universe. Picture each thread as a cosmic bond, linking you to people, places, and experiences. As you explore this cosmic fabric, see how each connection contributes to the vibrant patterns of your life. Embrace the cosmic interlacing of destinies, recognizing that every thread is an essential part of the intricate masterpiece of your existence.

15 Monday

Moon ingress Cancer is an excellent time for self-care and addressing your emotional needs. You may feel more intuitive and receptive to the emotions of those around you, making it a favorable period for fostering deeper connections in your relationships. Embrace the caring and compassionate energy of the Cancer Moon to create a warm and supportive atmosphere in your life, providing a solid foundation for emotional well-being and understanding.

16 Tuesday

Venus sextile Mars. It's a favorable time for romantic pursuits and relationships, as you exude a captivating energy that draws people towards you. This alignment supports creative endeavors as your passion and artistic expression find a natural rhythm. Embrace the synergy of Venus and Mars to embrace both the gentle and assertive aspects of yourself, making it a period of joyous connections and creative inspiration.

17 Wednesday

Moon ingress Leo. Mercury opposed Saturn. It's essential to be patient and not let any setbacks deter you from pursuing your goals. Instead, use this time to carefully plan and analyze your thoughts, ensuring your messages are clear and well-structured. Embrace the Leo Moon's vibrant energy to infuse enthusiasm and playfulness into your pursuits, and allow the Mercury-Saturn opposition to inspire you to think diligently and overcome any obstacles that come your way.

18 Thursday

As Mercury enters Libra, you may notice a shift in your communication style towards diplomacy and seeking harmony in your interactions. This astrological influence encourages you to consider various viewpoints and find common ground with others. However, with Mercury opposed to Neptune, there may be a tendency for misunderstandings. Being cautious with decisions or commitments is essential, as the Neptune influence can lead to unrealistic expectations.

19 Friday

You attract practical and organized pursuits as the Moon and Venus enter Virgo. This combination fosters a desire for efficiency and attention to detail, making it an ideal time for refining your daily routines and work processes. Embrace this period to nurture both your intellectual and practical sides, allowing for personal growth and fulfillment in your endeavors. It is an ideal period for promoting connections and focusing on acts of kindness that can strengthen bonds.

20 Saturday

Venus Square Uranus astrological alignment can bring a sense of restlessness and a desire for freedom and independence in matters of the heart. You might be drawn to unconventional or non-traditional relationships or encounter disruptions and surprises in your existing partnerships. It's essential to be open to new experiences and perspectives during this time and mindful of impulsive actions that could lead to instability.

21 Sunday

With the Sun opposed to Saturn, you may experience a sense of restriction or challenges that hinder your progress and self-expression. This astrological aspect can bring feelings of self-doubt or limitations in achieving your goals. However, you can start fresh as the New Moon graces the sky and the Moon moves into Libra. This lunar transit encourages you to find balance and harmony in your life, especially in your relationships and emotional well-being.

September

22 Monday

With Mars entering Scorpio, you may feel a shift towards a more intense and determined energy. This astrological event enhances your passion and drive, urging you to delve deep into your desires and motivations. As the September Equinox arrives, you experience a balance between day and night, symbolizing a time of equilibrium and reflection. It's a moment to reassess your goals and aspirations, seeking harmony and alignment with your inner self.

23 Tuesday

When the Sun is opposed to Neptune, you may experience a sense of confusion or uncertainty. This astrological aspect can bring a cloud of illusion, making it difficult to see things clearly or confidently make decisions. Your sense of identity and purpose might blur, and you may find it challenging to differentiate between reality and fantasy. Staying grounded and avoiding making important choices based solely on emotions or romantic notions is essential.

24 Wednesday

With Mars square to Pluto, there can be a potential for power struggles and conflicts. Managing any feelings of frustration or control is essential, as they can lead to unnecessary tension in your interactions. Embrace the Sun's positive energy in trine to Uranus and Pluto to welcome positive changes. Use the Scorpio Moon's influence to delve into your emotions with courage and authenticity and navigate the Mars-Pluto square with mindfulness and a willingness to transform.

25 Thursday

Imagine your life as a cosmic cauldron, bubbling with the alchemical energies of transformation. Envision the celestial elements swirling within, each experience and challenge contributing to the heavenly brew. Picture yourself as the alchemist, skillfully navigating the cosmic reactions, transforming the base metals of adversity into the golden wisdom of personal growth. In this cosmic laboratory, every trial becomes an opportunity for profound transformation.

26 Friday

As the Moon moves into Sagittarius, you may experience a surge of adventurous energy and a desire for exploration. This lunar transit inspires you to seek new experiences and expand your horizons. Your emotions become more optimistic and open-minded, making it a favorable time to learn and broaden your knowledge. Sagittarius' influence encourages you to embrace freedom and independence, urging you to break from routine and enjoy spontaneity.

27 Saturday

You soon lift the lid on an expansive journey that heightens prospects in your life. It brings a blossoming time of chasing your dreams and developing remarkable goals. It touches you down on an approach that promotes enrichment and progression. Lively discussions bring positive prospects that open the way toward developing longer-term goals. It brings an active and dynamic time that redefines what is possible in your life.

28 Sunday

Embrace the soothing lunar lullaby that cradles you in a cosmic hammock of reflection. Picture the moonbeams as gentle hands guiding you through the cosmic corridors of your memories and experiences. Envision yourself floating in this celestial cocoon, bathed in the soft glow of lunar introspection. As the cosmic cradle sways, allow your thoughts to dance in the moonlight, revealing the hidden depths of your soul.

OCTOBER

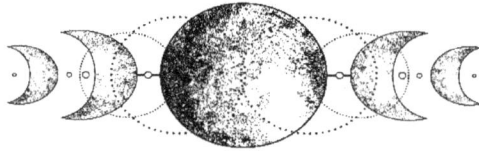

MOON MAGIC

Sun	Mon	Tue	Wed	Thu	Fri	Sat
			1	2	3	4
5	6	7	8	9	10	11
12	13	14	15	16	17	18
19	20	21	22	23	24	25
26	27	28	29	30	31	

NEW MOON

HUNTERS MOON

29 Monday

Moon ingress Capricorn. Capricorn's influence encourages you to focus on your long-term goals and responsibilities, seeking a sense of structure and stability in your emotions. During this lunar transition, you might be more focused on practical matters and determined to achieve your ambitions. The Capricorn Moon enhances your self-discipline and resilience, making it an ideal time to tackle challenging tasks and work diligently towards your objectives.

30 Tuesday

Picture the cosmic orchestra tuning up for a grand symphony of harmony in your life. Each celestial instrument, from the strings of patience to the brass of determination, contributes to the melodic rhythm of your cosmic journey. Envision yourself as the conductor, guiding these celestial notes into a harmonious crescendo that resonates with the cosmic vibrations of balance and tranquility.

1 Wednesday

As the Moon enters Aquarius, you may experience a shift towards a more open-minded and unconventional emotional outlook. This astrological influence encourages you to embrace individuality and think outside the box. However, Mercury square Jupiter has a potential for overly optimistic thinking and the tendency to overlook important details. This aspect can bring a sense of restlessness and a desire to take on more than you can handle.

2 Thursday

Wander through the celestial garden of creativity, where the cosmic blooms of inspiration await your touch. Envision each idea as a radiant blossom, bursting forth with vibrant colors and unique patterns. As you explore this heavenly garden, pluck the ideas that resonate most with your soul, weaving them into the tapestry of your creative expression. Let the cosmic petals of imagination bloom in the fertile soil of your mind.

3 Friday

Your social life hits a high point and triggers an active phase of mingling with friends. It brings music into your surroundings as thoughtful conversations draw happiness. It opens a perfect time to step out into a community environment and engage with others who support your life. Lovely changes nurture a lively and inspiring path ahead. It creates space for grounded foundations that draw peace and stability.

4 Saturday

You may experience heightened empathy and emotional sensitivity as the Moon moves into Pisces. This astrological influence encourages you to connect with your intuitive and compassionate side, making it a favorable time for self-care, artistic expression, and connecting with others on a deeper emotional level. Pisces' energy fosters a dreamy and imaginative atmosphere, urging you to explore your inner world and engage in activities that nourish your soul.

5 Sunday

You are in a time of transition that can feel unsettling as sensitive emotions rise to be released. It attracts a healing influence that reverberates around your life, enabling you to make peace with the past and understand what has gone before, which is all part of your life's journey. Releasing outworn areas draws a clean slate of potential into your life. It does bring movement and discovery ahead as a new situation takes shape.

6 Monday

As the Moon enters Aries, you may feel a surge of energy and assertiveness. This astrological influence encourages you to take the lead and pursue your goals with determination. Aries' energy fosters a sense of independence and a desire to initiate new projects or activities. Simultaneously, with Mercury moving into Scorpio, your thoughts and communication become more intense and probing. You may delve into more profound subjects and seek to uncover hidden truths.

7 Tuesday

The Full Moon and Mercury-Pluto square combination encourages you to embrace self-reflection and authenticity. Use this period to release emotional baggage and engage in open, honest dialogue, allowing for healing and personal growth. While the Full Moon reveals your inner landscape, the Mercury-Pluto square challenges you to communicate honestly and avoid confrontations, fostering transformative connections based on mutual respect.

8 Wednesday

Venus sextile Jupiter alignment enhances your social connections and brings a sense of warmth and generosity to your interactions. The combination of the Taurus Moon and Venus sextile Jupiter encourages you to embrace the beauty around you, enjoy heartwarming connections, and engage in activities that bring you a sense of fulfillment and happiness. It is a favorable time to nurture your emotional well-being and bask in the joy of the bonds you share.

9 Thursday

A curious assignment ahead lights up pathways of creativity and artistic expression. It brings a chance to take your gifts to a broader audience and link with a group environment that nurtures fresh possibilities in your life. Getting involved with kindred spirits brings the chance to cultivate friendships in a social setting. Communication flows as you spend time with others who resonate with your frequency.

10 Friday

With the Moon moving into Gemini, you might notice a shift towards increased curiosity and communication. This astrological influence encourages you to engage with the world around you through conversations, learning, and sharing ideas. Gemini's energy fosters versatility and a desire for mental stimulation, making it an excellent time to engage in intellectual pursuits and connect with others through engaging discussions.

11 Saturday

When Venus opposes Saturn, you may encounter emotional challenges and limitations in your relationships. This astrological aspect can bring a sense of distance or restrictions in heart matters. You might experience moments of self-doubt or find it difficult to express your feelings openly. It's essential to be patient and realistic, as this opposition can also prompt you to reevaluate the structures and commitments in your connections.

12 Sunday

With the Moon moving into Cancer, you may notice a shift towards a more emotional and nurturing state. This astrological influence encourages you to connect with your feelings and seek comfort and security. Cancer's energy fosters a deeper connection to home and family, making it an ideal time to spend quality moments with loved ones. Your intuition may rise during this lunar transition, allowing you to tap into your emotions and those of others with greater sensitivity.

13 Monday

With Venus moving into Libra, you may experience a heightened desire for harmony and balance in your relationships and surroundings. This astrological transition encourages you to seek out beauty and cultivate a sense of aesthetics in your life. Libra's energy fosters a focus on cooperation and diplomacy, making it an excellent time to work on resolving any conflicts or disagreements. You might enjoy social gatherings and activities that promote connections with others.

14 Tuesday

As Venus opposes Neptune, you may navigate a period of heightened romantic and artistic idealism. This astrological aspect can bring a yearning for deep connections and experiences that transcend the ordinary. Simultaneously, Pluto's direct motion encourages profound inner transformation and empowerment. As the Moon moves into Leo, your emotions become more expressive and enthusiastic, urging you to seek recognition and creative outlets.

15 Wednesday

As you sail towards smoother waters, it sets the tone for growing the potential possible in your life. It brings opportunities to use your inherent gifts to give back to a broader community and deepen your knowledge with new pathways that offer growth. Renewal and rejuvenation is a strong theme that restores your energy and gives you the nourishment needed to continue on this journey of developing your life.

16 Thursday

Moon ingress Virgo astrological transition encourages you to focus on details and organization, seeking efficiency and improvement in daily life. Virgo's energy fosters a strong sense of responsibility and a willingness to contribute through service and attention to others' needs. During this lunar transit, you might find satisfaction in tackling tasks and projects that require precision and careful planning.

17 Friday

When the Sun forms a square aspect to Jupiter, you may experience optimism and a desire for expansion. This astrological influence can bring a sense of enthusiasm and confidence, encouraging you to set your sights on grand goals and big ideas. However, be mindful of overextending yourself or taking on more than you can handle. The Sun square Jupiter energy can lead to a tendency to overestimate your capabilities, leading to potential challenges if not balanced with practicality.

18 Saturday

Pluto's transformative whispers echo through your experiences, signaling a period of profound change and evolution. Embrace the power of regeneration and allow the phoenix within to rise from the ashes. This cosmic phase encourages you to release old patterns and embrace the transformative potential of rebirth. This period enables you to recognize the creative power within, allowing it to shape a reality that reflects the desires of your soul.

19 Sunday

Moon ingress Libra astrological influence encourages you to seek balance and cooperation in your interactions with others. Libra's energy fosters a desire for fairness and social grace, making it an excellent time for connecting with friends and loved ones. During this lunar transit, you might find yourself more attuned to the needs and feelings of those around you, creating a more harmonious and pleasant atmosphere in your interactions.

20 Monday

With Mercury conjunct with Mars, you may experience heightened mental energy and assertiveness. This astrological alignment enhances your communication style, making your words more direct and potentially assertive. Your thoughts become more focused and driven, and you will likely express yourself more confidently. This conjunction can also bring a sense of urgency to your ideas and discussions, motivating you to take swift action.

21 Tuesday

New Moon. Moon ingress Scorpio. It is a favorable time to release what no longer serves you and embrace personal empowerment. Combining the New Moon and the Moon's ingress into Scorpio offers a powerful window for self-discovery and renewal. Use this period to set clear intentions aligned with your deepest desires and use the Scorpio energy to tap into your inner strength, fostering a period of emotional healing and personal growth.

22 Wednesday

With Neptune moving into Pisces, you may experience a heightened sense of intuition and a deeper connection to your inner world. This astrological transition brings a dreamy and imaginative energy that encourages you to explore your subconscious mind and embrace your spiritual side. Neptune's influence in Pisces fosters a sense of compassion and empathy, making it an ideal time to connect with others more profoundly and intuitively.

23 Thursday

As the Sun moves into Scorpio, you may notice a shift towards more intense and introspective energy. This astrological transition encourages you to delve deep into your emotions and explore the hidden aspects of your psyche. Scorpio's energy fosters a desire for transformation and rebirth, urging you to let go of what no longer serves you and embrace new beginnings. This period may bring heightened intuition and a stronger connection to your inner motivations.

24 Friday

On a bright note, the Mercury trine Jupiter adds a touch of intellectual optimism and enhances your communication skills. This alignment fosters a positive exchange of ideas and the potential for learning and growth. Embrace the Sagittarius Moon's energy to embrace exploration and the bigger picture while navigating the challenges of the Sun square Pluto aspect with courage and a commitment to personal evolution.

25 Saturday

When Mercury forms a trine aspect to Saturn, you may experience a period of increased mental focus and practical thinking. This astrological alignment enhances your ability to concentrate on tasks and communicate precisely and clearly. Your thoughts may become more disciplined and organized, allowing you to tackle complex subjects easily. This trine fosters a sense of responsibility and a willingness to plan, making it an excellent time for making important decisions.

26 Sunday

Moon ingress Capricorn astrological influence encourages you to focus on your responsibilities and set practical goals. Capricorn's energy fosters a disciplined approach to your emotions, urging you to manage them with maturity and a long-term perspective. During this lunar transition, you might focus more on your professional endeavors and seek to establish a strong foundation for your ambitions.

OCTOBER

27 Monday

Opportunity comes knocking and opens a journey that inspires progress around your life. It captures the essence of wanderlust as you develop a dream that promotes happiness. As you design the path and create progress around your life, you build more balanced foundations that offer heightened security and stability. Life opens to a vibrant landscape that redefines what you thought possible in your world.

28 Tuesday

With Mars forming a trine to Jupiter, you may experience increased energy, enthusiasm, and a sense of expansion. This astrological alignment empowers you with an optimistic outlook, encouraging you to take bold actions and confidently pursue your goals. Your drive and determination heighten, making it an excellent time to initiate new projects or endeavors that require ambition and careful planning.

29 Wednesday

With the Moon moving into Aquarius, you may experience a shift towards a more intellectually curious and open-minded emotional state. This astrological transition encourages you to embrace your uniqueness and engage with innovative ideas. As Mercury forms a trine to Neptune, your thoughts and communication take on a more intuitive and imaginative quality. This transit enhances your ability to tap into your creativity and connect with others deeply.

30 Thursday

With Mercury forming a sextile to Pluto, you may experience a period of intensified mental focus and profound insights. This astrological alignment empowers you to delve deeply into subjects that intrigue you and uncover hidden truths. Your thoughts become more perceptive and analytical, allowing you to grasp complex concepts quickly. This sextile encourages meaningful conversations and the potential for transformative communication.

NOVEMBER

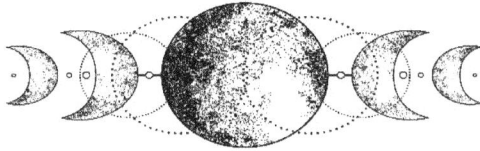

MOON MAGIC

Sun	Mon	Tue	Wed	Thu	Fri	Sat
						1
2	3	4	5	6	7	8
9	10	11	12	13	14	15
16	17	18	19	20	21	22
23	24	25	26	27	28	29
30						

New Moon

_____

_____

_____

_____

_____

_____

_____

_____

_____

_____

_____

_____

_____

_____

_____

_____

_____

_____

_____

_____

BEAVER MOON

31 Friday

Moon ingress Pisces astrological transition encourages you to tap into your intuition and embrace the subtle nuances of your feelings. Pisces' energy fosters empathy and a sense of oneness with others, making it an ideal time for compassion and understanding. During this lunar transit, you might find solace in creative pursuits or activities that allow you to express your emotions and imagination.

1 Saturday

Jupiter, the planet of abundance, bestows its blessings upon your journey. Open your heart to the expansive possibilities that life presents. This period encourages optimism, gratitude, and a generous spirit. Trust that the universe is conspiring to shower you with abundant blessings. You receive signs to help guide your path towards greener pastures. Creativity heightens, opening a time of nurturing your abilities and promoting your talents.

2 Sunday

As the Moon moves into Aries, you may experience a surge of energy and assertiveness. This astrological shift encourages you to take the initiative and embrace an independent and proactive emotional state. With Venus forming a square to Jupiter, there's potential for extravagant emotions and a desire for indulgence. This aspect can bring optimism and longing for pleasure, but it's essential to be mindful of overextending yourself or making impulsive decisions.

3 Monday

Life opens to a new flavor, bringing a journey worth savoring. Your career heads towards advancement and takes you on a journey that deepens your knowledge. You discover pathways that provide progress, leading to more significant success, which helps you achieve tangible results in your working life. Actively tapping into this journey helps grow your career outwardly. It brings assignments suitable for progression as you land in a landscape ready to blossom.

4 Tuesday

The Mars-Uranus opposition adds an element of unpredictability and potential disruptions to your actions. Embrace the Mars-Neptune trine to infuse your endeavors with magic while utilizing the Sagittarius energy to expand your horizons. As the Taurus Moon promotes stability, strive for a balanced approach to change, and heed the Mars-Uranus opposition's call to find innovative solutions as you navigate this dynamic and transformative period.

5 Wednesday

The Full Moon astrological phase reveals what is hiding, allowing you to see things clearly and gain insights into your feelings and situations. This lunar transition is a time of realization and revelation, where emotions can run deep and relationships or situations can come to a turning point. The energy of the Full Moon encourages you to release what no longer serves you and to embrace transformation and growth.

6 Thursday

Embrace the Mars-Pluto sextile's energy to initiate positive changes and tap into your inner strength. While navigating the Gemini Moon's influence, embrace curiosity and open-mindedness in your interactions. The Venus-Scorpio influence encourages you to embrace your passions and seek authenticity in your connections. Use these energies collectively to engage with life's complexities and foster meaningful relationships while pursuing personal growth.

7 Friday

Opportunities ahead broaden your circle of friends. Your life heats up with new possibilities as you get a glimpse of the path forward that gets you on track to develop your dreams. People enter into your life, bringing a new energy that cultivates change. You reveal a fresh chapter of your life that connects with a vibrant landscape of possibility. It links you with companionship that brings happiness and joy.

8 Saturday

With Uranus moving into Taurus, you may enter a phase of gradual yet potentially profound change in your life. This astrological transition encourages you to embrace innovation and explore new ways of approaching stability and security. As Venus forms a square to Pluto, there's potential for intense emotional experiences and power dynamics in your relationships. This aspect urges you to examine the depth of your desires and confront any hidden issues that may arise.

9 Sunday

Mercury's retrograde astrological phenomenon encourages you to review your plans, projects, and interactions. During this time, misunderstandings and technical glitches might become more prevalent. It's advisable to double-check your communications, contracts, and travel arrangements. While Mercury is retrograde, you might find it beneficial to slow down and focus on completing unfinished tasks rather than starting new endeavors.

10 Monday

As the Moon moves into Leo, you may notice a shift towards a more expressive and confident emotional state. This astrological transition encourages you to embrace individuality and shine in the spotlight. Leo's energy fosters a desire for attention and appreciation, prompting you to engage in creative endeavors and enjoy moments of self-expression. During this lunar transit, you might seek activities that bring you joy and allow you to showcase your talents.

11 Tuesday

As Jupiter turns retrograde, you enter a period of introspection and inner growth. This astrological phenomenon encourages you to reflect on your beliefs, aspirations, and broader sense of purpose. During this retrograde phase, you may discover that opportunities for expansion and abundance may come from within as you revisit past experiences and seek more profound understanding. It is a time to reassess goals and consider whether they align with your authentic self.

12 Wednesday

Mercury conjunct Mars. Moon ingress Virgo. This combination encourages you to engage in tasks that require precision and attention to the finer points. Embrace the Mercury-Mars conjunction's energy to express assertively and make decisive choices while allowing the Virgo Moon to enhance productivity and analytical thinking. Use these cosmic influences to effectively communicate intentions and tackle tasks enthusiastically and efficiently during this dynamic period.

13 Thursday

Your life brightens as you embark on growing your world. It opens a journey bursting at the seams with refreshing potential. Happy changes ahead give you what you need to move towards expansion. It connects with friends who offer supportive discussions and advice. A unique cycle draws a welcome boost of invitations for your social life. It offers an upgrade that brings the room to expand your circle of friends.

14 Friday

The Moon, a celestial mirror of emotions, reflects your internal landscape. As it journeys through its phases, embrace the opportunity for introspection. Tune into your feelings, allowing them to guide you through the cosmic currents. The moon's phases mirror the cyclical nature of life's emotional tapestry. It prompts introspection and regeneration. Embrace the metamorphosis, recognizing that every transformational phase brings you closer to your authentic self.

15 Saturday

As the Moon moves into Libra, you may notice a greater emphasis on balance and harmony in your emotions and interactions. This astrological transition encourages you to seek fairness and cooperation in your relationships. Libra's energy fosters a desire for companionship and a willingness to find common ground. During this lunar transition, you might find yourself drawn to social activities and engaging in conversations that create understanding and unity.

16 Sunday

The sun, a cosmic powerhouse, radiates dynamic energies into your life. Bask in the solar glow and harness the vitality it provides. This period supports your physical well-being and personal growth. Embrace the warmth of the sun as it illuminates your path with clarity and purpose. A unique possibility lets you pass the threshold and head towards greener pastures. It opens a happier phase of developing areas that inspire you greatly.

17 Monday

With the Sun forming a trine to Jupiter and Saturn, you may experience a period of balance between expansion and stability. This astrological alignment empowers you with a sense of optimism and discipline. It's when you can progress on your goals with a practical yet positive mindset. As Mercury sextiles Pluto, your communication gains depth and insight, allowing you to engage in meaningful discussions and uncover hidden truths.

18 Tuesday

Bask in the warm glow of the solar embrace, a cosmic illumination that guides you on a journey of self-discovery. Picture the sunbeams as heavenly fingers gently lifting the veil of self-awareness. Envision yourself in this celestial radiance, casting aside shadows to reveal the brilliance of your true essence. In the solar embrace, embrace the transformative power of self-discovery, allowing your inner light to shine brightly in the cosmic constellation of existence.

19 Wednesday

With Mercury moving into Scorpio, you may experience intensified and probing communication. This astrological transition encourages you to uncover hidden truths beneath the surface. As Mercury opposes Uranus, there's potential for unexpected shifts and disruptions in your thoughts and interactions. This aspect can lead to sudden challenges in finding common ground. The Mercury-Neptune trine adds a touch of intuition and creativity to your communication style.

20 Thursday

Embrace the New Moon's energy to initiate positive changes and set intentions that resonate with your desires while allowing the Sun-Mercury conjunction to align your thoughts with your goals. Let Mercury in Sagittarius inspire you to seek knowledge and embrace the influence of the Uranus-Neptune sextile in fostering a balance between innovation and imagination during this period of fresh starts and mental exploration.

21 Friday

With the Sun opposed to Uranus, you may experience a period of unexpected disruptions and the urge for change. This astrological aspect can bring about sudden shifts in your routines and a desire to break free from limitations. However, the Sun's trine to Neptune adds a more harmonious and creative influence. This alignment encourages you to tap into your intuition and imagination, finding inspiration from within.

22 Saturday

As the Sun moves into Sagittarius, you may feel a shift towards a more adventurous and optimistic energy. This astrological transition encourages you to embrace a broader perspective and seek new horizons. With Mercury forming a trine to Saturn, your thoughts and communication become structured and focused, enabling you to tackle tasks precisely. As the Moon moves into Capricorn, your emotions may take on a disciplined and determined tone.

23 Sunday

Sun sextile Pluto astrological alignment empowers you to make meaningful changes and tap into your inner reservoir of strength. The Sun's energy blends harmoniously with Pluto's intensity, encouraging you to delve and uncover hidden truths. This sextile fosters a positive synergy between your willpower and capacity for change. Embrace the Sun-Pluto sextile's energy to harness your power and initiate transformations in areas that may benefit from renewal.

24 Monday

With Mercury taking center stage, intellectual pursuits come to the forefront. Your mind is a powerful tool during this period, so engage in stimulating conversations, express your thoughts, and explore new ideas. The cosmic intellect is in your favor, promoting clarity and effective communication. Let your inner light shine, illuminating the path ahead. Trust in your uniqueness, and allow the cosmic rays of the sun to guide you toward personal fulfillment.

25 Tuesday

With Mercury forming a conjunction with Venus, you may experience enhanced communication and a focus on relationships and harmony. This astrological alignment empowers you to express your feelings and thoughts with charm and grace. Your interactions may become more pleasant and engaging, making it a favorable time for connecting with others on a deeper level. As the Moon moves into Aquarius, your emotions may become more open-minded.

26 Wednesday

With Venus forming trines to Jupiter and Saturn, you experience balanced energy in love, relationships, and values. This astrological alignment empowers you with abundance and stability. The Venus-Jupiter trine encourages expansion and growth in matters of the heart, fostering an optimistic approach to your connections. Meanwhile, the Venus-Saturn trine adds a practical and grounded influence, promoting commitment and long-lasting bonds.

27 Thursday

On Thanksgiving, as the Moon moves into Pisces, you may experience a shift towards a more compassionate and empathetic atmosphere. This astrological transition encourages you to embrace the spirit of gratitude and connect with your emotions more intensely. Pisces' energy fosters a sense of unity and a willingness to give and receive love. It's a favorable time to come together with loved ones and reflect on the blessings in your life.

28 Friday

As Saturn turns direct, you may experience a shift in the energy of responsibility, structure, and discipline in your life. This astrological phenomenon signals a time when obstacles that may have felt like they were holding you back could begin to lift. Saturn's direct motion encourages you to take practical steps toward your goals and build a solid foundation for your future endeavors. It is a favorable period for making long-term plans and setting realistic objectives.

29 Saturday

With Mercury turning direct, you may experience a sense of clarity and a lifting of the communication fog. This astrological event marks the end of a period when Mercury appeared to be moving backward, potentially causing misunderstandings, delays, or miscommunications. As Mercury resumes its usual forward motion, you can expect smoother interactions and greater ease in conveying your thoughts and ideas.

30 Sunday

Moon ingress Aries astrological transition encourages you to embrace a sense of independence and a desire for action. As Venus opposes Uranus, there's potential for unexpected disruptions or changes in matters of the heart and finances, which can either bring excitement or unsettle you. However, with Venus trine Neptune, your relationships and desires take on a more compassionate and dreamy quality, inviting you to connect on a deeper emotional level.

DECEMBER

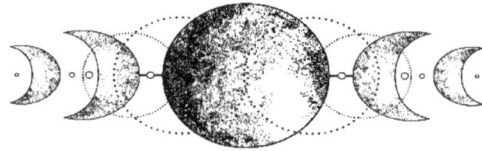

MOON MAGIC

Sun	Mon	Tue	Wed	Thu	Fri	Sat
	1	2	3	4	5	6
7	8	9	10	11	12	13
14	15	16	17	18	19	20
21	22	23	24	25	26	27
28	29	30	31			

New Moon

COLD MOON

1 Monday

A cosmic dance between assertiveness and cooperation is underway. Find a healthy equilibrium between standing your ground and collaborating with others. Be mindful of power dynamics, and channel your energy into constructive outlets. This period encourages a dynamic interplay between individuality and teamwork. Communication flows effortlessly, and mental agility becomes a powerful asset. Seize the opportunity to express yourself with clarity and precision.

2 Tuesday

With the Moon moving into Taurus, you may seek comfort, stability, and a sense of groundedness. This astrological transition encourages you to appreciate simple pleasures and indulge in sensory experiences. As Venus forms a sextile to Pluto, your relationships and desires may take on a deeper, more transformative tone. This aspect fosters an opportunity for profound emotional connections and passionate encounters.

3 Wednesday

Cosmic forces encourage a harmonious blending of tradition and innovation. Embrace change while respecting the wisdom of the past. This period offers an opportunity to navigate the dance between stability and progress, finding unique ways to integrate old and new elements in your life. This period invites you to explore profound spiritual insights and expand your understanding of the world around you.

4 Thursday

As the Moon moves into Gemini, you may feel a more communicative and intellectually curious state of mind. This astrological transition encourages you to engage in conversations, seek information, and explore various ideas and perspectives. With the arrival of the Full Moon, emotions may come to a climax, highlighting areas that require attention and resolution. It is a potent time for reflection and releasing what no longer serves you.

5 Friday

Jupiter's expansive energy fills the cosmic canvas with optimism and hope. This period encourages a buoyant outlook on life. Look beyond immediate challenges and focus on the vast landscape of possibilities. Trust that, under Jupiter's benevolent gaze, opportunities for growth and abundance abound. Explore new territories, whether mentally, physically, or spiritually. This period supports educational pursuits and the pursuit of knowledge.

6 Saturday

With the Moon moving into Cancer, this astrological transition encourages you to connect with your innermost feelings and create a safe space for emotional expression. Cancer's energy fosters a sense of compassion and domesticity, making it an ideal time to spend with loved ones or engage in activities that bring solace. Additionally, with Mercury forming a trine with Neptune, your communication takes on a more intuitive and empathetic quality.

7 Sunday

The Moon's journey through the zodiac highlights emotional resonance. Trust your instincts and allow your emotions to guide you. This period favors intuitive understanding. Listen to the whispers of your heart as you navigate the cosmic currents. Whether it's partnerships or friendships, cosmic forces invite you to delve into the intricacies of connection. Take this time to understand the give-and-take in your relationships, fostering harmony and mutual growth.

8 Monday

Striking a balance between professional pursuits and personal well-being takes center stage. Cosmic energies encourage you to evaluate your work-life dynamics, ensuring that your endeavors align with your passions and contribute to your overall sense of fulfillment. Seek harmony in your daily routines as it opens a unique and original journey that feels the right fit for your life. It helps lift the fog and improves life with grounded foundations that nurture balance and stability.

9 Tuesday

With Mars forming a square to Saturn, you may experience frustration and obstacles. This astrological aspect can bring about a sense of limitation and a need to work diligently to overcome challenges. You might encounter delays in your pursuits, which can be frustrating. However, this cosmic alignment is a valuable lesson in patience and discipline. While this aspect can be challenging, it also offers an opportunity to build resilience and strengthen your determination.

10 Wednesday

The Mercury's opposition to Uranus adds a touch of unpredictability to your thoughts and communication, potentially leading to sudden insights or changes in plans. Embrace the Virgo Moon's energy to tackle tasks with precision and attention to detail, and use Neptune's direct motion to tap into your intuitive side. Navigate the Mercury-Uranus opposition with adaptability and an open mind, allowing it to inspire innovative solutions and creative thinking.

11 Thursday

Mercury trine Neptune astrological alignment empowers you with fluidity and imagination in your thinking and communication. Your thoughts become more attuned to the subtler aspects of life, making it a favorable time for artistic endeavors, spiritual exploration, and empathetic conversations. As Mercury moves into Sagittarius, your thinking becomes more adventurous. Allow this cosmic synergy to inspire intellectual pursuits and bring wonder and curiosity.

DECEMBER

12 Friday

As the Moon moves into Libra, you may notice a shift towards a more harmonious and balanced emotional state. This astrological transition encourages you to seek fairness and cooperation in your interactions with others. Libra's energy fosters a desire for companionship and a willingness to find common ground. During this lunar transit, you might find yourself drawn to social activities and engaging in conversations that create understanding and unity.

13 Saturday

With Mercury forming a sextile to Pluto, you may find that your thinking and communication take on a profound quality. This astrological aspect empowers you to explore and express ideas and insights with a heightened intensity and focus. It's a favorable time for engaging in conversations that delve beneath the surface and uncover hidden truths. You may also find that your ability to research and investigate complex matters is particularly sharp during this period.

14 Sunday

When Mars forms a square aspect with Neptune, you might face frustration or confusion in your actions and ambitions. This astrological alignment can make asserting yourself and taking decisive steps toward your goals challenging. Neptune's dreamy and illusory influence can cloud your judgment and lead to misunderstandings or misplaced efforts. It's essential to be cautious during this time, as it can be easy to become entangled in unrealistic or deceptive situations.

15 Monday

As the Moon enters Scorpio, you may sense a shift towards intense and passionate emotions. This astrological transition encourages you to delve deep into your feelings and explore the hidden aspects of your psyche. Scorpio's energy fosters a desire for transformation and a willingness to confront emotional complexities. Additionally, with Mars moving into Capricorn, your actions and ambitions are more disciplined and goal-oriented.

16 Tuesday

Exploring the potential on the periphery of your environment lights up pathways of connection and support. You reveal an area that inspires your imagination as it brings personal development to the forefront. As you make notable tracks in improving your life, you cast your net of dreams and come up with a winning trajectory. A new realm of possibilities tempts you forward and brings harmony into your life.

17 Wednesday

With the Sun forming a square to Saturn, you may encounter a sense of restriction and obstacles in your path. This astrological aspect can bring about challenges and delays, making it feel like your ambitions are met with resistance. It might be when responsibilities and limitations seem particularly prominent, casting a shadow over your confidence. However, as the Moon moves into Sagittarius, you'll find a spark of optimism and a desire for adventure.

18 Thursday

The current astrological alignment fosters celestial harmony in your relationships. Focus on creating a balance between giving and receiving, nurturing the bonds that bring joy and fulfillment. Allow the cosmic energies to infuse your connections with a sense of mutual understanding and shared growth. You attract an environment that is soul-affirming and enriching as you mingle with friends and enjoy more company and companionship in your landscape.

19 Friday

Celestial alignments infuse your words with a touch of magic. Express yourself with eloquence and engage in meaningful conversations that transcend the ordinary. Your thoughts have the power to inspire not only yourself but those around you. Communication becomes a conduit for creativity and inspiration. Engage in lively conversations and let the exchange of ideas flow effortlessly. This period favors mental agility, making it a time for expressing with eloquence.

20 Saturday

It's a period when you may be drawn to explore profound truths and seek a deeper understanding of the world around you. Embrace the New Moon's energy to set clear intentions aligned with your desires and aspirations. Utilize the Capricorn Moon's influence to plan and work diligently toward your goals. Let the Black Moon's presence in Sagittarius inspire your spiritual and philosophical explorations as you navigate this phase of new beginnings and personal growth.

21 Sunday

As December Solstice transitions into a new season, you'll notice the days growing longer or shorter, depending on your hemisphere, bringing a shift in the rhythm of life. With the Sun's ingress into Capricorn, you're encouraged to embrace a more structured and disciplined approach to your goals. While the Sun-Neptune and Venus-Saturn squares may bring uncertainty, the Capricorn Sun prompts you to focus on building solid foundations and persevering in the face of challenges.

22 Monday

Moon ingress Aquarius. During this lunar phase, you might find yourself drawn to humanitarian causes and a sense of camaraderie with like-minded individuals. Use this cosmic alignment to break free from routine and embrace opportunities for personal growth and collective progress. The Aquarius Moon's influence invites you to approach your emotions with an open heart and a spirit of curiosity, allowing you to navigate with authenticity and positivity.

23 Tuesday

The cosmic orchestra plays a symphony of harmony, inviting you to attune yourself to the celestial vibrations. Find resonance in the balance of cosmic energies, fostering a sense of alignment and peace within. This period encourages you to synchronize with the universal rhythm and embrace the interconnected dance of existence. Tune into the lunar cycles to gain a deeper understanding of your feelings and inner rhythms. You can navigate the tides of emotion with grace.

24 Wednesday

With Venus forming a square to Neptune, you may find that matters of the heart and your perceptions of beauty and harmony are veiled in a certain mystique. This astrological aspect can bring about a sense of idealism and romanticism, but it's crucial to exercise caution in relationships and financial matters during this time. Simultaneously, as Venus moves into Capricorn, your approach to love and values takes on a more practical and goal-oriented tone.

25 Thursday

It's a time for kindness, reflection, and a heightened sense of unity with those you cherish. Whether you celebrate with family or spend the day in quiet contemplation, allow the Pisces Moon's energy to inspire acts of kindness and gestures of love. Christmas becomes an opportunity to share the warmth of your heart, offering a sense of solace and connection, reminding you of the power of compassion and the importance of cherishing the bonds that bring joy.

26 Friday

Uranus, the planet of change, sparks the fires of liberation within. Embrace your individuality and welcome the unexpected. This period encourages you to break free from routine, inviting innovation and a bold departure from the norm. Unleash the liberating energy of Uranus and embrace the thrill of the unknown. Events on the horizon bring new possibilities. It kicks off a lively time that nurtures happiness. It marks the turning point as the changes ahead get the magic flowing.

27 Saturday

Moon ingress Aries. During this time, you may be motivated to pursue your goals and overcome obstacles enthusiastically. It's an opportune moment to channel this fiery energy into productive endeavors and to take initiative in areas of your life that could benefit from a bold and confident approach. Use this cosmic influence to fuel your passions, ignite your inner drive, and tackle challenges with courage and determination.

28 Sunday

As the celestial bodies align in a tranquil dance, a sense of cosmic serenity envelops your being. It's a period to find solace in the gentle rhythms of the universe. Take moments for self-reflection and connect with the quiet wisdom that resides within. This cosmic hush encourages you to listen to the whispers of your soul. This period enables a symbolic rebirth, allowing you to emerge more substantial and more aligned with your true self. Trust the unfolding cosmic plan.

29 Monday

You might appreciate life's pleasures, from indulging in delicious food to taking in the beauty of the natural world. Use today's cosmic influence to create a peaceful and nurturing environment for yourself, allowing your senses to revel in the sights, sounds, and textures that bring you solace. The Taurus Moon invites you to slow down, savor the present moment, and find tranquility in life's simple pleasures as you navigate this period with calm and contentment.

30 Tuesday

Mercury square Saturn. You might find it difficult to express your thoughts and ideas clearly, as Saturn's restrictive influence can create barriers in your communication style. This aspect often brings a sense of self-doubt and can lead to overthinking, making it challenging to trust your judgment. Finding a balance between being cautious and allowing yourself to express your thoughts confidently is crucial.

31 Wednesday

As the Moon ingresses into Gemini on New Year's Eve, you'll likely feel a shift in your emotional energy. Gemini, an air sign ruled by Mercury, is known for its quick-wittedness and communicative nature. Under this influence, you may be more inclined to engage in lively conversations, connect with friends, or explore new ideas and interests. Your emotions could become more adaptable and changeable, mirroring the dual nature of the Gemini sign.

1 Thursday

On New Year's Day, Mercury ingresses into Capricorn; while forming a square aspect with Neptune, you might encounter challenges in communication and decision-making. Your thoughts may feel foggy, and expressing yourself clearly or making practical plans for the year ahead can be challenging. Neptune's influence can bring a dreamy and imaginative quality to your thinking, but it may also lead to misunderstandings or miscommunications if you're not careful.

Astrology, Tarot & Horoscope Books.

Mystic Cat

Mystic Cat Tarot

In Relationship Reading
$15.00

Crossroads
$10.00

Next Relationship Reading
$15.00

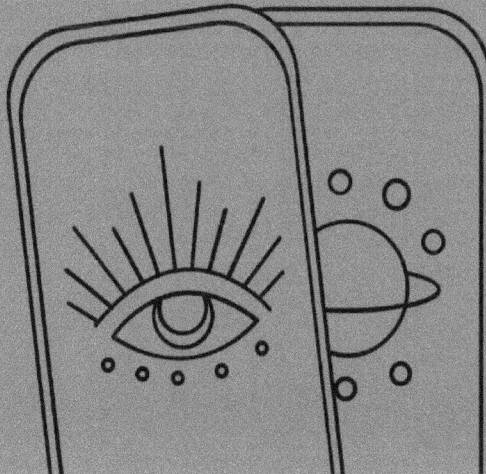

Ohoroscope@Hotmail.com